Build a Brand in 30 Days

Build a Brand in 30 Days

Simon Middleton

The Brand Strategy Guru

CAPSTONE
be inspired!

This edition first published 2010
© 2010 Simon Middleton

Registered office
Capstone Publishing Ltd. (A Wiley Company), The Atrium, Southern Gate,
Chichester, West Sussex, PO19 8SQ, United Kingdom

For details of our global editorial offices, for customer services and for information
about how to apply for permission to reuse the copyright material in this book
please see our website at www.wiley.com.

Library of Congress Cataloguing-in-Publication Data

9781907312427

A catalogue record for this book is available from the British Library.

Set in Meridien Roman 10/14 by aptara
Printed by TJ International Ltd. Padstow, Cornwall

Praise for Simon Middleton

"Simon Middleton has years of experience helping companies understand more about their brands. He is extremely creative in his approach."

— Jay Chapman, Head of Communications, Pret A Manger

"Simon has a great knack of asking the right questions and a terrific talent for getting to the essence of something, persevering to cut out all woolly thinking until you are left with the great 'aha!' moment."

— Fiona Reid Wilson, Head of UK Intranet, AVIVA

"Simon has a passion for great branding, great customer experience, and excellence per se. His recent work on 'brand purpose' is at the cutting edge of what organisations need to be engaged in."

— Darren Cornish, Head of Customer Experience, AXA

"Simon is a rare breed - a genius and a superb communicator with an infectious enthusiasm for his subject matter."

— Gordon Maw, founder MAW Communications

About the author

*Author photograph by
Claudia Gannon*

Simon Middleton, The Brand Strategy Guru, has worked with world-class brands including Barclays, Aviva, pharmaceutical giant Merial, and sandwich 'superbrand' Pret A Manger. As a specialist independent brand adviser he has advised numerous businesses, charities and public sector organizations and is currently helping Hemsby, one of Britain's smallest seaside resorts, to put its brand profile on the world tourism stage.

Simon writes and presents *The Brand Effect*, the first TV series to look in depth at brands and branding on British television. Simon presents master classes and keynotes in the UK and beyond. He is a regular media commentator on all things brand related, and in 2009 he became the first Brand Leadership Fellow at the University of East Anglia.

Simon trained as a primary school teacher but found himself instead as a writer and business magazine editor, then a PR executive. He retrained as a nurse, working with people with severe learning disabilities, and spent almost a decade in the NHS. After a second career as an advertising copywriter and creative director, he launched his own brand and creative consultancy practice in 2005.

When he's not advising on brands, Simon fuels his creative energy by writing for and fronting acoustic Americana band 'The Proposition'.

To Sheila, obviously.

Acknowledgements

It's been a long time coming, this book, and many of the people who have influenced it may have slipped from my memory (at least at this uncomfortable moment of trying to remember all those to whom thanks are owed). Forgive me if you're not on this list.

First, thanks to all the entrepreneurs, business and organization leaders and specialist experts who gave their wisdom and experience in these pages (some of whom I'm proud to count as clients as well as friends):

Andy Wood of *Adnams*, Bea Hatherley of *Mr Site*, Brian Horner of *Voluntary Norfolk*, Caroline Rust of *WorkShopsWork*, Chris Murphy of *Balloon Dog*, David Keeling of *bpha*, David Knights and Robert Spigel of *Anthony Nolan*, Fiona Ryder of *StreamExchange*, Gordon Maw of *Maw Communications*, Jay Chapman of *Pret A Manger,* singer-songwriter Jess Morgan, Mark Cook of *Further*, Sarah Pettegree of *Bray's Cottage Farm*, Scott Poulson of *Special Design Studio*, Simon Egan and Tom Blofeld and John Lyle of *Bewilderwood*, Stephanie Diamond of *Digital Media Works*, and *Aviva* corporate storyteller Tracy Kenny.

Thanks to those who contributed to making this book happen, including my agent Seamus Lyte, my publisher Emma Swaisland, my editor Jenny Ng, and Scott Poulson for the cover.

Thanks to those people who have played a role (probably larger than they realize) in helping me to understand what branding and, indeed, entrepreneurship are really about, by allowing me to prattle on to them, interrogate them, work with them, argue with them and be inspired by them over the years. They include: Jay Chapman,

Chris Murphy, Steve Turton, Alison Brown, Scott Poulson, Lucy Marks, Paul Thomas, and Fiona Reid Wilson. Thanks to Nik Coleman for enabling me to get some of my ideas on the telly. Thanks to James Gray in Hemsby for helping me start a new journey into destination branding. Thanks to nation branding expert Simon Anholt (*il miglior fabbro*) for the best advice I've ever received. And thanks to Alan Weiss for setting the bar so very high and inspiring me from the beginning of the solo journey.

Thanks to those close to me who, though wise enough to know that there is more to life than branding, have nevertheless always supported me in my obsessive interest. Top of the list are my wife and best friend (and my best personal brand advisor) Sheila, and my proudly individual children Paul and Alice. Next my Mum, whose intelligence, fierce zest for life and unbridled energy have always been an inspiration. And to my Dad, a writer, painter and hopeless romantic who knew that it isn't what you sell that counts, but what you struggle to create.

Thanks also to my irreplaceable compadres of so many years in 'The Proposition' and other musical endeavours, Nigel Orme and Steve Clark. Also to Liz, Maddy and Sheila again, for letting us play at being rock stars for nearly two decades.

"God made man because He loves stories."

Yiddish proverb

Contents

Introduction

How this book works

Do you know anything about brands or branding? No? That's perfect. Know a little or a lot about branding? That's fine too.

This book is designed to work whether you are starting completely from scratch (i.e. you know nothing at all about branding and you have zero background in anything to do with branding or marketing) or if you're already something of a brand expert. This book takes a stripped down, no-nonsense, non-academic approach which I hope you'll find stimulating, enjoyable and useful.

This book is both a general introduction to the powerful, exciting and effective craft of branding and a process which you can follow, one day at a time, for 30 days. Follow the programme, and by the end you will have transformed your understanding of branding and how it works. And along the way you will have created a powerful and sustainable brand for your business or organization (or even for yourself as an individual).

To sum up, you can use this book to:

- Educate yourself fast in the art of branding

- Actually build a proper brand for your business or for any of its products or services

- Build a brand for a charity or public sector organization

- Build a brand for your team or department within a bigger organization

- Build your own personal brand in order to enhance your career

And to explain the '30 days' of the title: each chapter represents a key stage of the branding process, and each of those stages can be initiated and achieved in a single day.

Some of these days will be more intensive and longer than others, of course. But if you are able and willing to commit 30 days of thinking and doing, then by following the steps in this book you will create a proper brand which will be more powerful, more effective and more sustainable than you could possibly have hoped to achieve by virtually any other means.

I'm not suggesting for a second that you start on the 1st of the month and finish with a loud "Hurrah!" on the 30th. You won't want to do every stage back-to-back. And I wouldn't advise it. You're much more likely (and more likely to be successful) to spread the 30 days over, say, three months. The exact timescale is up to you. But don't rush it. Brands, like puppies, should be for life, not just for Christmas. At least, if not for life, then for a substantially long period of time, so nothing is gained by rushing the process.

Each 'day' is designed to take you through an important stage which requires some reflection. And on many of these 'days' you'll come across a challenging 'Brand Builder Workout' (an exercise which demands some self-examination and active thinking). Interwoven between the days and their workouts you will also find inspiring Real Brand Stories from people who have created successful brands both large and small, and Expert View pieces on a range of specialist topics from search marketing to employee engagement.

So, 30 days of reading and thinking and 'exercising', but spread over a longer period (I recommend about three months, but it all depends on your style and your schedule). And three months or so from now you will have created a brand which will outperform anything that could have been built without the knowledge in this book.

Day I

What Your Brand is and What Your Brand isn't

There are lots of misconceptions about brand and branding and what these terms actually mean. For some people these terms are veiled in a kind of arcane mystery, as though 'brand' was exclusively the province of specially qualified executives in huge and complex companies. For others the words 'brand' and 'branding' are inseparable from other specific aspects of marketing, such as advertising, logos, and slogans. Yet others think of branding as a dark, mysterious and probably evil art, practised by the hidden persuaders of capitalism.

But brand isn't really about any of these things. Brand isn't a subset of advertising (it's actually much more important than that). Brand isn't your logo. And it shouldn't be complex or mysterious.

Brand is serious and important to your business: but it's also very simple in its essence. **Brand is about meaning.** In short, **your brand is the sum total of all the meanings that all your possible audiences carry around about you in their heads and in their hearts.**

In other words, your brand is everything that your customers and prospective customers think, feel, say, hear, read, watch, imagine, suspect and even hope about your product, service or organization.

Take the British store John Lewis. Ask any group of people in the southern half of the UK what John Lewis 'means' (and I know because I've asked numerous workshop audiences over several years) and you will discover that most people share a fairly small number of 'meanings' for John Lewis.

Regardless of background, level of affluence, and whether they shop in John Lewis or not, the following meanings are always mentioned within the first minute or two of starting this exercise: quality, service, value, partnership, middle class.

This is not to say that these are the only words used. Of course not, but no matter how often I repeat the exercise these five meanings are the dominant ones: in fact they are the 'headline' meanings under which almost every other idea about John Lewis can be put.

Some people will say "John Lewis staff are always polite", which of course falls under Service. Others will remember the store's long-standing slogan "Never knowingly undersold", which reflects the brand meaning of Value.

Interestingly, most people are familiar with the fact that John Lewis is a partnership organization: in other words that each of its staff 'own' a little bit of the business. Materially this doesn't matter to us, the shopper. But philosophically, somehow it does. I think it's because we feel somewhere deep inside that if this store is in partnership with its employees then that indicates a value system which will in one way or another translate into a better relationship with us. We become a kind of partner of John Lewis too, just by shopping there: which is not the feeling one gets in most stores.

Not all the meanings that groups throw up in this exercise are positive. 'Middle class' is descriptive and neutral in and of itself, but is actually loaded with value judgements, most — though not all — on the negative side.

The negatives for John Lewis under the Middle Class headline include descriptions like: boring, stuffy, old fashioned, a bit posh. Some people go on to say "it's not for me" and "it's not really a family store", and "it's expensive".

But alongside these interpretations, John Lewis is also seen as aspirational and appealing, even to those people who call it stuffy, boring and posh.

The point overall is that John Lewis as a brand has a definable meaning which is almost all positive (quality, service, value) and that even its few negative meanings actually have a positive aspect. After all, even 'boring' is a reassurance that things will be just as you expect, every time. John Lewis is therefore much more than a name or a logo, or a number of big stores with certain stock. John Lewis 'means' something.

One more example. Draw the Nike logo (which, curiously, everyone seems to know is called the 'swoosh') on a piece of paper and people instantly respond with a whole new set of meanings. Nike head-line meanings usually amount to the following: achievement, sport, design/technology, fashion, quality, expense, high-profile sponsor-ship figures (exemplified by Tiger Woods), hip-hop culture, child labour/sweatshops.

Nike has somewhat more complex meanings than John Lewis for two reasons. First, it's an international brand with a massive adver-tising and sponsorship spend. Second, it works across cultures to many different audiences.

Once again, you'll see on the list one brand meaning which is obviously not a desirable one for Nike. The interesting thing about 'child labour' as a brand meaning is that it is historic rather than current; however, it is a very powerful meaning, and one that Nike will have to live with for decades to come regardless of their actual labour practices.

Nike is a fascinating case of brand meaning. One might say that Nike is a brand and nothing else. The fact that Nike can be simultaneously so successful and yet so insubstantial as an organization is the most powerful evidence in retailing of the power of brand as meaning. And the fact that it is so multi-faceted as a brand (even though it markets a fairly narrow range of goods) demonstrates that brand is not a static thing but an ever-changing and dynamic one.

Why does this matter? Why does brand meaning matter so very much to Nike, to John Lewis, to any other brand you can name? And why should it matter to you?

Well, the answer is that without 'brand' John Lewis would be just a department store, and Nike would be, well, not much really. It is brand that gives these two businesses a personality and presence in the world. It is brand that enables us to understand them, and allows them to communicate with and sell to us.

Brand is a kind of shorthand. A way for a business or a product to introduce itself to people (customers and potential customers). But brand is also a kind of tool for those customers to use when making buying decisions.

When we choose a pair of trainers or decide which department store to shop in, we don't make the choice rationally, at least not completely rationally. That would be impossible, because the world is too complex. And even an apparently simple decision like which department store to visit when, say, looking for a new fridge, is fraught with difficulty.

Do we really have time to compare every single feature and benefit of every make and model of fridge in every different store? Let alone to cross reference that information with prices, guarantees, special offers, delivery charges and so on. And what is our ideal fridge decision anyway? How do we know when we've made the best rational choice?

The fact is that we don't have time or head-space, or even the information processing capacity to make these decisions rationally. So instead **we use a system of signs and meanings that have come to be known as 'brand'.**

If we've registered John Lewis in our internal system as a brand that we trust to give us quality, service and value, then we don't have to make anywhere near as many difficult decisions. Plus, of course, we remember the John Lewis promise of being 'never knowingly undersold', which overcomes our anxieties about them being expensive.

Funny thing about this slogan, too. When John Lewis say it, we believe it, because they are a trusted brand. It wouldn't be difficult to name a dozen retailers from whom we wouldn't trust that statement.

There's one more crucial element to remember from the beginning about brand: it's not about size. It is perfectly possible to be a brand with just a few dozen loyal customers. You can be a local chip shop and be a great brand. It's not the absolute numbers of people who know about you that make you a brand, but the relative coherence of what they think, feel and believe about you.

If you have 100 customers who share a set of meanings about your business then you've got a strong brand. If you've got 10,000 customers who don't have a shared set of meanings then you have a weak or non-existent brand.

"So what," you might say, "I've got 10,000 customers... so who needs a brand?"

Good question, but the answer is simple. Ten thousand people might buy from you this week or this month, but if you haven't engaged them as a brand (given them some meaning), then there's no particular reason for them to buy from you again. They might do. But they might just go somewhere else.

But if you have a strong brand, a strong set of meanings, then your 100 customers will come back, again and again. Because your brand helps them to make their buying decisions easier. And not only will they come back, but they'll tell others about you too.

Brand gives you stability, growth potential, loyalty and longevity.

Consider the alternative. If you don't have a set of meanings that works for customers both rationally and emotionally, then where does that leave you? You might say it makes you a commodity. Just a set of functions rather than a set of meanings.

You can survive in business as a commodity. Lots of businesses do. But it's tough. Because if you're a commodity then you had better be cheaper, quicker or more convenient than your competitors, because that's what you will be judged on. As a brand, however, cheapness, speed and convenience are much less critical factors because, as a brand, you tap deeper into human psychology. As a brand, you go beyond a functional 'transaction' with your customers, and they start to buy from you because you somehow fit in their world and what it means to them.

It's a very powerful and enviable place to be. Big business understands it (although sometimes they get it terribly wrong). Many small businesses don't apply themselves to building brands anywhere nearly as much as they could or should. But you can, and I'm going to help you.

This book can't make your business into John Lewis or Nike. Because they are unique and so are you. But what it can do is guide you through the process (and the state of mind) of brand and branding, so that you can develop a set of brand meanings that are positive and attract people to come to you, to stay with you and (the ultimate brand benefit) recruit others to come to you, too.

Whether you're a flower shop or a financial adviser, a designer or a gardener, a charity or a voluntary organization, a local council or a wedding planner, a chip shop proprietor or a car mechanic, if you follow my steps you can become a powerful and sustainable brand.

Brand Builder Workout

Bearing in mind the concept of brand as sets of meanings (e.g. Nike and John Lewis), try to list the meanings of two of your favourite brands here.

Brand name:

Meaning 1: _____

Meaning 2: _____

Meaning 3: _____

Meaning 4: _____

Meaning 5: _____

Meaning 6: _____

Brand name:

Meaning 1: _____

Meaning 2: _____

Meaning 3: _____

Meaning 4: _____

Meaning 5: _____

Meaning 6: _____

Now, here's your first big brand challenge: repeat the exercise with your 'brand' as it stands now. And for this to be valuable, you need to be very honest. Don't write down a meaning that is just wishful thinking on your part. Try to put yourself in the shoes of your customers. If you can't (or won't) do that, ask a friend whom you trust, and insist that they are brutally honest. Better still, ask a customer!

Your brand:

    Meaning 1: _____

    Meaning 2: _____

    Meaning 3: _____

    Meaning 4: _____

    Meaning 5: _____

    Meaning 6: _____

This is just the start. We will revisit this exercise later on, and if you follow the steps in this book you'll be amazed at the difference in results.

Day 2

YOUR BRAND BENCHMARK TEST

We've established an idea of what a brand is, and what a brand isn't. Remember, it hasn't got that much to do with your logo! Before we go any further, let's take a look at your brand as it stands now, to try to establish whether it's yet become a brand and, if so, whether it's one that is working effectively.

The simplest of all benchmarks of your brand is to think about how it performs on two measures: strength and positivity.

Take a look at the diagram below. It's one of those simple four box grids created by two axes.

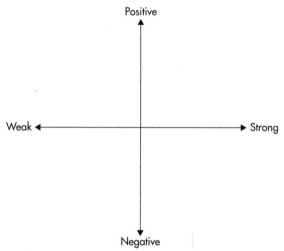

Measuring brand positivity and strength.

The horizontal axis is a measure of the strength of your brand, from weak to strong. Far left of the axis is where the weakest of brands sit, far right is for the strongest. But what are the characteristics of weak and strong brands?

Weak brands are characterized by any combination of the following:

- few people know about the brand

- few people understand what the brand is about or there are mixed messages and mixed perceptions about the brand

- brand knowledge is limited to a small geographic area (i.e. smaller than the business requires)

- people can't remember the name

- you have to explain at length what your brand is about before people say "Oh, right, got it now"

- your business has changed emphasis (speciality, positioning, products, services, pricing, ownership, personality) but your old customers don't realize

By contrast, strong brands are characterized by any combination of these elements:

- a substantial number of people know about the brand (the definition of 'substantial' will vary according to your circumstance: if you own a neighbourhood chip shop then 'substantial' for you will be different in size and scope to someone running an online kids' clothing brand)

- the majority of the people who know about the brand will share a common set of meanings and perceptions about it (they don't all have to think exactly the same, but there will be general agreement)

- brand knowledge is widespread (right across the neighbourhood for the chip shop, or widely spread amongst parents wanting to buy kids' clothes online)

- people remember the name (and lots of them remember the positioning line, i.e. the 'slogan')

- you don't have to explain over and over what your brand is about, people just seem to know

- if the brand has changed its emphasis, the perceptions about the brand have changed also: new customers are catching on quickly and old customers have kept up with the changes and understand what you're about today

Of course, most brands won't sit at one extreme end or the other of the strong–weak axis: it's a spectrum. I don't know your brand, of course, so only you can decide where to place your brand on this axis. Have a think for a moment, but don't settle on anything yet — we'll come back to it shortly.

Strength and weakness represent only one measure of a brand and if you look at that measure alone you could easily deceive yourself about the real situation.

So you'll see that the diagram has a second measure, positivity. The vertical axis ranges from negative at the bottom to positive at the top. It is very common indeed for people in companies to mix up positivity and strength. They are not the same thing and we need to treat them quite differently.

Just by way of example, think about countries as brands. Take the two Koreas. North Korea has a very strong brand, based on our criteria above. People all over the world have an idea of what North Korea is 'about', and can summon up a number of visual images and impressions as well as words and descriptions. Sadly, for the time being at least, those brand perceptions, whilst strong, are not positive. They include the perception that the nation is poor and isolated from the world community, and the people repressed by a totalitarian government. We can picture images of enormous statues of 'the great leader', and TV coverage of elaborately choreographed military parades. South Korea, by contrast, has a much more positive brand image, but arguably a much weaker one. Unless we have visited there we are likely to be much less clear in our minds about what characterises South Korea as a nation, although we are also less likely to carry 'negative' brand perceptions around in our heads about the country. In the West, South Korea is seen as much more developed and affluent than North Korea, and a democracy into the bargain. But most Westerners don't have a clear picture in their minds of what South Korea looks and feels like (compared to perceptions of Japan, for example).

But enough about countries for the moment. Let's think about whether your brand sits at the top (positive) end of the vertical axis or at the bottom (negative) end.

Negative brands are characterized by some very simple (but not very good) characteristics, as follows:

- people are more inclined to complain than to praise (but watch out for this one, by the way: the old cliché is true that people are more likely to tell you when they're happy and others when they're not!)

- when your brand comes up in conversation that conversation is generally focused on what your brand gets wrong

- you get little, if any, repeat business unless you are competing aggressively on price or convenience or are maintaining a very high profile through advertising (simple example, if you're a very conveniently placed shop or hotel with competitive pricing, then you may well get lots of customers; you could be deceived into thinking they all like you, but you may just be either 'cheap' or 'handy')

- no matter how hard you try with advertising or other marketing efforts you don't seem to be attracting repeat business (or even that much valuable new business either, come to that)

- customers are not recommending you to others and you rarely, if ever, have new customers say to you "my friend Sam recommended that I come to you"

By contrast, positive brands will be characterized by some combination of the following:

- people spontaneously thank you or compliment you on your service, product or some aspect of their experience of dealing with your brand (this one is a bit like being in love… you'll know it when it happens!)

- your brand is always praised and celebrated when it comes up in conversation ("Oh yeah, those guys **are great**, you have to try them")

- you get lots of repeat business and those **repeat** customers start to buy a wider range of products/services from you, and they return more frequently

- you're not spending heaps of money on advertising, but you seem to have created some kind of 'pull' and new customers seem to appear from nowhere

- when you ask them, it turns out that a substantial proportion of your new customers have had a recommendation: "Oh yes, my friend Sam thinks you're great and said I should come here"

Just like the weak–strong axis, the negative–positive one is not a black-and-white or cut-and-dried issue. It's a spectrum, and only you can decide where your brand currently sits along it.

Brand Builder Workout

Before you try placing your brand in the right place in our quadrant, try placing some other brands that you know about.

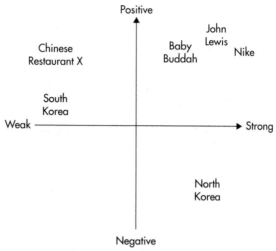

John Lewis looks to be very well placed.

You can see where I've placed John Lewis and Nike, and where I've put North Korea and South Korea.

I've also put in two Chinese restaurants from my city (I haven't named one because that wouldn't be fair). You can see that one, Baby Buddha, is not just a strong brand but also a very positive one, and the other is weak but positive. They have above-average service and very good home-produced Cantonese-style food. But one of them is, sadly, frequently empty and only known by people who happen to live near it, whilst Baby Buddha (a small family-run restaurant) is causing a real buzz: people are telling other people about it, commenting on it, praising it and returning to it. Heck, it even gets a mention in a branding book!

It's important to remember here that this way of measuring brands is not absolute but relative. Which is why Baby Buddha can have a similar place on the chart to John Lewis. And that's why this method works for your brand, too.

Think about where you would instinctively place the following brands on the grid:

Your local convenience store

Your favourite pub or café

McDonalds

The (not so new now) New Mini

Manchester United F.C.

The National Health Service

The BBC

Sainsbury

Tesco

Now I recommend that you try this same exercise with your competitors. **Whatever kind of brand you're building, you have competitors, and they may not always be the ones you think.** I was recently outflanked by a completely unexpected competitor. A prospective client came to me and asked for a proposal for a substantial piece of brand strategy consultancy. The brief was exclusively about 'strategy' and was to involve a deep and extensive examination of the organization's brand 'meaning'. My ideal client, in fact. Several meetings and one detailed proposal later, the organization appointed a design company instead. And that's what I mean by your competition coming from unexpected quarters. So never fall into the trap of thinking that you don't have competitors. For now, though, just try to place your competitors on the grid. And think about how they sit in relation to one another even if they are in the same quadrant: is one a little more positive than another, or a little weaker perhaps?

Now it's the turn of your brand.

But because it's your brand and therefore you know everything about it, you can afford to be a little more analytical. You also need to be ruthlessly honest with yourself.

So before you place yourself in the grid (in fact, we're going to use a new grid with numbers, just to be a little more methodical), ask yourself these questions and score yourself 1 to 10 (10 being a brilliantly positive answer to the particular question, 1 being an honest admission of a negative answer).

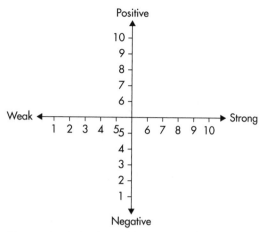

Give your brand a strength score and a positivity score and plot it on the grid.

Ask yourself these simple brand strength/weakness questions, and give yourself a score for each one.

- Do sufficient people know about my brand (10) or is it pretty much unknown and/or invisible (1)? ☐

- Do people always remember its name (10) or does it frequently get confused or forgotten or just doesn't seem to have registered with people at all (1)? ☐

- Do the people who know about it understand thoroughly what the brand is about (10) or am I always having to explain it to people (1)? ☐

Now add your scores together and divide by 3 to get an average score out of 10.

Average score   ☐

Now plot your brand somewhere along the horizontal axis line of the previous grid using your average score. For example, if your average score from the three questions is 8, then you'll be about half way along the right-hand side of the horizontal axis. If your average score is only 2, then you'll be almost at the far left of the left-hand side of the same axis.

Now for the positive/negative scoring. Again some simple questions:

- Do I hear mountains of compliments and praise about us and what we do (10), or does it feel like people are constantly griping and grumbling (1)?   ☐

- Are people always telling me that they've heard good things about my brand (10), or do I not get any feedback like that at all (1)? (by the way, lack of feedback equates to negative feedback, because your friends don't like to give you bad news)   ☐

- Do I get a lot of repeat customers and new people seeking me out (10), or does it always seem such an expense and effort to attract people (1)?   ☐

- Are people always saying that their friend recommended me to them (10), or does that just no t happen (1)? [Again, add your scores together, this time dividing by 4 to get an average score out of 10.   ☐

Average score   ☐

- This time, plot your brand somewhere along the vertical axis line of the grid, using your average score. For example, if your average score from these four questions is 6, then you'll be just above the horizontal line, whereas if you get a high average, say 9.5, you'll be very close to the top.   ☐

Whatever your average score, you'll end up with two marks, one on each line. So to find your proper place in the grid, mark an X where the two marks meet, as shown in the previous example.

Now think about where you sit on the grid compared to your competitors that you placed on the previous grid. Do you look good next to them? Or are you a bit disappointed or downhearted? Don't be, we're only on DAY 2!

The important things to remember about this exercise are:

- for it to be of value you have to do it honestly, but don't beat yourself up unnecessarily

- trust your instincts: this can never be scientific and whatever you intuitively feel is right is more than likely to be so

- don't rely entirely on your own view: try asking others (friends, family, employees, shareholders, customers, even complainers) to give their scores of your brand

///

And before we close this chapter, a final word about why this strength/positivity exercise is so important for small (and developing) brands. Imagine that your brand is both strong and positive. Maybe it already is, which is wonderful. Whatever you're doing, keep doing it. You're going to be fine. Now imagine that your brand is (for reasons which you don't yet fully understand) apparently pretty negative. Lots of complaints, difficulty retaining and attracting customers, etc.

If you've got a negative brand image, think about this: would you rather it was a strong-negative image, or a weak-negative? Well, no prizes for guessing which one I'd say is the most challenging. **Strong brands are great when they're positive, and a major hassle when they're negative,** because people's perceptions are hard to change, and the more people involved, the bigger the problem.

So you need to know, right off the bat, where your brand sits in the quadrant. And once you know, here's a shorthand guide to what needs to be done:

- Strong/Positive (top right-hand quadrant): keep on truckin'.

- Weak/Positive (top left-hand quadrant): people really like you, so tell more people.

- Weak/Negative (bottom left-hand quadrant): put the negatives right first, before you do anything on the 'more people' front.

- Strong/Negative (bottom right-hand quadrant): oops, you're in the toughest place of all, but don't panic, just keep reading, we can sort it out!

Day 3

FINDING YOUR AUTHENTIC PURPOSE

People who spend time with me know there are two words that I am prone to use more than any others, and these are: **brands** and **purpose**.

The **brand** word won't surprise you at all, of course. But perhaps **purpose** is a little more oblique. I'll explain where I'm coming from with **purpose** (and that's the last time I feel the need to put it in bold), and why it's so important to your business or organization and your brand. Come to that, why it's so important to you as a human being, let alone as an entrepreneur.

When I say purpose, I'm talking about the motivation behind what we do. The reason we jump out of bed in the morning wanting to make something happen that's different to, or better than, or an exciting development of, what we made happen yesterday. Nobody goes into business just to make money. Well, maybe they do, but that drive to make money will usually yield up a deeper purpose or drive when it's examined in any detail. Not that there's any shame in making money. At least in part it's what business is about: by definition. But there is something beyond the money.

But the big question is: what's your business here for? What is its purpose?

Answering this existential question is a core part of the process of building a brand: what's different about it that makes it more compelling, more sustainable and more successful than your competitors? Answering this will help you create something infinitely more robust and more effective in the marketplace than any amount of advertising, or PR or any other marketing tool or activity alone.

In future chapters we're going to explore purpose from different angles, and we'll go through a number of steps to help you identify and build upon your purpose. Every single step will help you make a better brand. In this chapter I just wanted to introduce you to the concept of purpose and to explain briefly each of its eight special elements.

You'll meet each one again as you read on through the book. Remember though, this isn't a hierarchy or a linear list. The elements of purpose are all interdependent, all equally important to your brand. I call them the eight building blocks of brand purpose.

1. *Ambition and desire* Ambition and desire are about what you personally want from this endeavour. They're about your emotional needs and your need for personal fulfillment. They might include material desires, of course, and I'm always worried when I meet start-up business people who say they're not interested in making money. Frankly, that's a dangerous thing not to be interested in when you're starting a business. But it's unlikely to be just material or status needs that drive you. Most people have needs relating to a host of other aspects of their humanity. Think about what your 'personal' needs are in setting out on this brand journey. In fact, don't just think about them, feel about them too.

2. *Talent* Talent is important in many ways but it's important to clarify what we mean by talent. I absolutely don't mean that you have to have an exceptional skill or a 'gift' in order to be a successful business owner and brand-builder. Talent for our purposes does include an honest assessment of your skills and abilities, but it also refers to the people whom you will need to gather around you (either as employees or occasional helpers). Talent refers also to your own personal development needs. You may need to up-skill in certain areas, for example. Most importantly of all, though, talent is about creating a business and a brand that suits the person you are: a brand which somehow expresses and utilizes your mix of abilities and interests.

3. *Rational intent*   In contrast to the emotional aspects of your personal ambitions and desires, your brand purpose also needs a big healthy dose of rational intent; by which I mean an understanding and a clarification of where you're planning to go with this enterprise. It's closely related to the well-worn concepts of goals and objectives. But rational intent focuses on what you 'decide' to do rather than just making lists of things you ought to do. You can't make a business or a brand without rational intent. You can have dreams all right, but without applying the rational then dreams they will remain.

4. *Values*   The principles and concepts that guide your behaviour and your decision making, values play a vital role in developing your brand. Values are the things you won't compromise. And **if there's nothing you will not compromise, then you will never make a brand that is distinct, compelling and authentic** (and great brands need to be all three of those).

5. *Context*   Simply a word to describe what's going on around your brand in the wider world. It includes your obvious competitors, of course, but it also includes whatever is competing for your customers' attention and spending which might not seem so obvious. Context includes the spirit of the time, whether optimistic and outgoing, or pessimistic and inward looking. Your context is also a function of geography, politics, history, ethnicity, social structure and other factors. Complex though it is, context is a huge influence on the success or otherwise of a brand. All brands exist in the context of the world in which they operate. There is no such thing as a pure brand operating in a vacuum.

6. *Creation and imagination*   Brands are never built by numbers alone nor, contrary to the popular belief of so-called 'marketing experts', are they created by identifying a need and finding a way to fill it more effectively or more cost-effectively. That's just

not what happens in our complex economic world and our even more complex internal and social worlds. It's true that products and services which are utterly useless and outrageously inappropriately priced are going to struggle (though there are plenty of examples of brands that succeed even though they fit completely within this description). But the truth is that building a brand is absolutely as much an act of the imagination as it is a rational process. The best piece of business advice I was ever given was this: **"never put a limit on your ambition and imagination for there will be plenty of people who will try to do that for you."** And it's advice which I commend to you as a brand-builder.

7. *Narrative*   There's no power in branding greater than the power of narrative or story. I believe that in many ways brands are our modern equivalent of folk-tales, the myths and legends that help us to understand, organize and narrate our complex and confusing world. We humans love nothing more than story. It reassures us, challenges us, draws us both out of ourselves and into our innermost beings simultaneously, and allows us to share experiences, dreams and concepts with all those other 'unknowable' people out there. Brands that use the power of story have a huge advantage over the rest. We will uncover and unleash your unique brand story.

8. **Resources**   It's easy to think of resources as material, or at least as measurable. Things like money and working space and equipment are obvious resources of this kind. But a brand-builder needs a huge range of other resources to work with, too. Resources like time and 'headspace' to investigate and pursue research, ideas and product/service development. Resources like resolve, resilience, and the ability to weather disappointment and criticism. Resources in the form of a committed team and supportive family and friends.

As you progress through this book you will see how to examine and develop each of these eight elements in order to create a real sense of purpose in your brand.

Brand Builder Workout

It's a very simple task this time. Over the next 24 hours or so, I just want you to think about what your 'purpose' is in building a brand. There's no right answer, and I don't want you to be too analytical at this point. Just ponder what the big picture is for you. Why are you embarking on this journey? But don't sweat it: we'll get down to the nitty gritty soon enough.

Day 4

Ambition and Desire: What Do You Actually Want From This?

People start businesses for a whole host of reasons, and it's not difficult to identify the key motivators:

To make a living (perhaps even a really good one)

To be 'independent'

To create, face and rise to a challenge

To achieve a better work–life balance

To achieve 'fulfillment'

To leave a legacy for our children

To make a mark on the world which can be identified as ours

To get rich

To achieve 'success'

To utilize one's special skills

To live according to one's most powerful passions

I could go on. And of course this list doesn't apply only to entrepreneurs (I'm using the word 'entrepreneur' to cover anyone who chooses to work for themselves, from freelancers to the creators of extensive businesses). It also applies to people working for others, in companies, charities, and in the public sector.

In fact we could change the opening sentence of this chapter to read: 'People strive to change and improve things in their work for a whole host of reasons.'

Although this book is primarily created for people starting or running small businesses, the lessons of branding remain as true, powerful and useful to those who head a team, or who have a leadership role in any kind of organization: not just the leadership role of Chief Executive, Managing Director or other senior position, but any kind of team leadership role, or any role relating to marketing, communications and the reputation of the organization.

Your brand might be your team within a much larger organization, or the small charity, public sector department, or medium-sized enterprise for which you work.

Whatever the circumstance, your brand is vital to the success of your enterprise, and you need first to understand and then apply its power. At the beginning, though, and this is the thrust of this chapter, you have to do some self-examination.

Brands (even the big, famous, rich brands) were at some point the creation of either an individual or a small group of people. Brands are not produced by machines, or by computers, or even by research. No, brands are made by humans and it's their inherent humanity which makes them so very powerful. **We respond to the best brands because they capture some aspect of our humanity and reflect it back to us;** because they work much more with our emotions than with our rational judgement.

You've already benchmarked where your brand is now, and before you think any more about where your brand needs to be, you need to examine *yourself,* that is you personally, the human behind the brand.

In particular, you need to look at your motivations: the forces that drive you to work late into the evening on your brand. And you also need to look at your goals. In other words, you need to ask where exactly you are hoping, wishing and planning for your brand to go in the future.

But why are these things so important? Because they will influence, heavily, what you do with and to your brand. In fact, they will play a decisive role in determining the kind of brand that you create and how you go about bringing it to life.

My guess is that you are reading this book because you are either considering starting a business, or in the process of doing so, or your business is at some kind of fork in the metaphorical road. In other words, it's 'decision time' in some way (growth, sale, change of direction, new product development, etc...). Or if you're working for a company or organization, the same 'decision time' imperative will probably also apply.

The great Yogi Berra, baseball icon and author, is often quoted as saying: "When you come to a fork in the road, take it." I couldn't agree more, but the following little exercises should help you take the right (or left) one.

Brand Builder Workout

Two exercises today! Give yourself a couple of hours and get stuck in.

There are no right or wrong answers to the following questions. Only honest or dishonest ones, and self-aware or self-deluding ones.

It's easy to do: for each question just choose from the four options the answer that most sounds like the authentic you, and make a note of your choice.

If you had to choose one of the following lifestyle descriptions, which would it be?

A. Work is work. Free time is free time. I want to do my job well. If a good brand helps then that's a bonus.

B. I'm up with the lark, totally focused on work throughout the day, but my evenings and weekends are sacrosanct, for myself and/or family. It's all about balance. I'm not defined by what I do.

C. I'm completely passionate about what I'm doing. It just doesn't seem like work because I love it so much, so I guess the boundaries are a bit blurred; there are no 'working hours' in the conventional sense.

D. I do what I do in order to give me the money, and the time, to enjoy my life. I work to live, not live to work. It's not money for money's sake, but it's certainly about a high level of independence and freedom that comes from money.

How do you 'feel' about your brand and its future?

A. I don't really 'feel' that much: I just want to learn about how to make the brand work effectively and simply.

B. The brand is really important because it assures the success of the business (team, organization) but the brand isn't 'me'. It's a tool.

C. The brand reflects my personality. It's not about me but I've created it and nurtured it and I care very much about how it is perceived and how it is looked after by others.

D. The brand works, so it has a valuable role in building value in the business, quicker than could be achieved otherwise.

What would you like to see happen to your brand eventually?

A. No strong feelings. If it's saleable that's great, but I'm really interested in it working now to provide a good living.

B. I'd like it to reach a sufficiently strong place where it might be viable to sell it on to senior people in the team who would run it and develop after me.

C. It's hard to imagine not being involved in the brand in some way.

D. It would be great to build it to a position where it could be sold to a larger company or investors, giving me a healthy reward as quick as possible for all the hard work.

What about the idea of developing another brand after this one, how does that feel?

A. Yep, that's a possibility. But one thing at a time.

B. Definitely interested in that thought, but I really want to make sure this brand is strong, healthy and moving in the right direction first.

C. Yes, because this brand is so exciting, and the challenge so stimulating that I'm already having ideas about the next one. Maybe a brand that reflects a different aspect of my personality and interests.

D. If this one makes money, then why not? On the other hand, if it makes serious money then I've plenty of other things I want to do.

Your answers

You'll have seen a pattern here: it's not far below the surface. If you answered mostly As then that would indicate that the brand (of your business, product, team, organization) is really a functional device for you. You have a lot to gain by understanding how your brand can be built and how it can work: but I think you might benefit from getting closer to the 'heart' of your brand, which this book will help you to do. **Brands are fundamentally about emotion. If you don't 'love' your brand, who will?**

If you answered mostly Bs then you're better placed to manage your brand personally. Your brand can (and I'm sure will) be a great success. But your slightly distant relationship to the brand might still mean that the business and the brand would benefit by engaging an individual to champion the brand (just so it doesn't get lost in all the other aspects of your business).

If you answered mainly Cs then you already understand a key truth about branding: that it is fundamentally an emotional activity. Brands speak 'to' the emotions of customers and other audiences, and they are most likely to do that effectively if they speak 'from' the heart of the brand owner and his or her team. Clearly if you chose mostly **C**s then you have an instinctive grasp of this truth and you're going to be passionately involved in your brand; but that doesn't mean that you don't face a challenge. It's just a different challenge, which is that you might find yourself too close to the brand, too hands-on, too controlling, especially as your brand grows. In some sense brands are like children. They have to fly the nest at some point, so you need strategies to ensure that you can proudly and calmly watch them take off. More of that later.

If you answered mainly Ds then you clearly have the drive to succeed, which is essential for brand success, and clearly you're not going to waste your time with a brand that isn't working. That's good. You'll be tough and focused. But you might be tempted to go for the short-term solution and you have to be wary about this when dealing with a brand. Building a brand doesn't always equate to maximum sales now; it can mean sacrificing some success now in order to build to longer success. There's nothing wrong with trying to use a brand to build a business rapidly, in order to sell it for some serious dosh. Plenty of people have done that. But it's also true that brands, like horses, can be driven too fast and too hard. And, like horses, they can become lame.

Time to get specific: sit right down and write yourself a letter

Psychologists know that it's much easier to describe something that has already happened than to describe something that is going to happen in the future.

For some reason, it's just much easier to describe things in the past tense. It's one of the reasons why most people find it so difficult to answer those horrid interview questions like: "What do you see yourself doing in five years' time?" Everybody hates those questions, not because we don't all have dreams and ambitions, some of which might be crystal clear in our internal world, but because they are so difficult to render into words and sentences without somehow losing their reality. Trying to describe the future can be like trying to describe a dream.

But somehow, before we can go much further with creating your brand, it is important to capture that vision of the future which is skipping dreamlike through your head.

One way to do this quickly and effectively is to write yourself a letter from the future. It's not a new idea, but I've used it many times to capture the emotional and imaginative aspects of brand-building; and it works. Here's how.

It's something you might want to do completely in private. And whether you ultimately share it with others in your team is up to you. You might want to take the 'facts' that emerge and share those, or you might want to inspire others with your rich personal vision. That's what I recommend, but really it's up to what suits you personally.

So, grab yourself a notebook or an A4 pad (I'd urge doing this by hand rather than on the computer, just to slow your writing down to allow your thoughts the time not to have to rush).

You are simply writing a letter, to yourself. Mine would begin, "Dear Simon".

Put a date at the top which is two, three, four or five years in the future. Now just describe from this future perspective what's going on in your life and business. Whom have you just hired? What kind of premises are you working in? Which products or services have taken off? Which have turned out to be disappointing and have either been dropped, re-configured or sold off? What's actually piled up on your desk right now (right now in the future, that is)? How will you spend the rest of your day? Where are you going when you finish work today?

Don't forget to describe your family and friends, your successes and failures over the past few months and years. What does your business look like now? What's the competition like? Have you achieved some of your ambitions? What challenges remain to be conquered?

You get the idea. Something about this act of describing the future as though it had already happened makes it come to life more vividly and more profoundly than any amount of more formal (and drier) 'planning' or 'forecasting'.

Of course, once you've written your letter (or letters; you might enjoy this process so much that you write a sequence of letters from different dates, or covering differing topics or aspects of your life and business), then you need to leave a little space for reflection.

Are there elements which have come out in your letter writing that alarm you? Things about your life in the future that make you wary or anxious or give you pause for thought? Are there elements of your future-reality which excite you more than others? Things you'd rather be doing than the things you'd previously thought you were aiming to do?

That's all good, because it will give you a richer perspective on where to go with your brand and help you to make good decisions when we get to the 'strategy' stage.

Don't be afraid to be imaginative and to tap into your emotions in this exercise. Remember, businesses and brands are made by humans for humans. Imagination and emotion, and the ability to picture the future, are all elements that define our humanity and make us into brand-creators and brand-consumers.

Now, who will be your brand champion?

If you've answered the four questions above honestly and considered your answers, and if you have written your letter(s) from the future, then I think you'll see that you have a number of important decisions to make before getting deeply into the brand work itself.

And please don't be impatient to get past this stage. It's really important. Brands are reflections of humanity. Brands have personalities, express emotions and have emotional impact. Sorting out up-front where you are coming from as the brand creator will save all kinds of problems later on and will substantially enhance your chance of brand success.

The first big question to answer is: are you the right person to 'create' the brand? It's not a value-loaded question. If the answer is 'no' or 'I'm not sure' that doesn't mean that you won't build a very successful business or, indeed, a successful brand. It may mean, however, that you would be wise to share this book and the experience of reading it with a trusted colleague/partner/employee to whom you can give the challenge of helping you create the brand.

And remember, even if you are absolutely the right person to create, launch and champion the brand, there may come a time in the future when you'd be wise to bring another brand champion to the fore. And it's worth looking out for and developing that person (or persons) from as early on as possible.

Just to clarify, when I say 'brand champion' I mean the person whose role it is to look after the brand, to tell the brand stories, to fight the brand's corner so it doesn't get lost in the business or organizational melee, to protect its values, its reputation, and ultimately its meaning.

Maybe you are indeed the ideal champion for your brand. Maybe not. But someone needs to have the role, and I believe that role should be publicly, formally and proudly announced. The brand champion role is one of the most important in any brand-savvy business or organization. It may not be the full-time job of an individual (small businesses are of necessity full of multitaskers) but it does need to be a role with prestige and clout!

So the second big question: if it isn't you, how do you go about choosing someone? My recommendation is to take your likely candidate through this whole book, working with you to develop your brand ideas together. But do let them have a voice and a serious input into the process and don't ever make the mistake of overruling them on the grounds that it's your brand, or indeed your company. I've seen that happen and it's not just demotivating for the junior party, it can sow the seeds of destruction in a brand or a whole business.

If you decide to share or delegate the brand responsibility, then you have to do so wholeheartedly.

The rest of the book assumes it is speaking to the 'brand champion'. It might be you (which would be nice). It might be your appointed champion (which will be fine). It might be both of you for now (which, frankly, is my recommendation).

Day 5

From Personal Ambitions to Rational Intent: Brand Strategy

Okay, Brand Champion, you've now established some idea of what you want from your brand and your business. You've got the evidence too; honest answers to difficult questions, and at least one letter from the future describing how you imagine things working out over the coming years.

All of this work has been unapologetically emotion- and imagination-based, as I've explained. And don't let any old 'business adviser' (or your accountant or your bank manager) tell you that emotion and imagination have nothing to do with starting or running a small (or, come to that, large) business. They have everything to do with it. And if you're serious about building a brand, not just a business, then they are absolutely vital. You simply can't do authentic branding without them.

But (and it's a big but): you must also combine all that emotion and imagination with a strong dose of rationality and analysis. That's what we're going to do in this chapter.

Day 5 in your 30-day programme is all about 'strategy'. We'll start with taking a closer look at the 'strategy' word, which I admit to having been scared of for years (it sounds so terribly serious, doesn't it?). The battered Chambers dictionary on my shelf defines strategy rather narrowly and militarily as: *generalship, or the art of conducting a campaign and manoeuvring an army.* The military definition is completely appropriate in a sense, of course, because the word itself derives from the Greek word for 'general', and that in turn from two words meaning 'army' and 'to lead'.

So strategy is about leadership. And in some way it's also about decisions in demanding circumstances (war or battle), and it's almost self-evidently about victory (or success, if you prefer). Not many generals deliberately lead their armies to defeat, although clearly lots of them have led their armies there by negligence, or ignorance, or lack of skill, or in some cases by bad luck or because of external circumstances over which they had no control.

As a brand champion, you are just as vulnerable to external circumstances as any general, ancient or modern. Sometimes the externals will appear to give you an edge. Sometimes these elements (what the Ancient Greeks might have said were the gods) will appear to be aligned against you.

It would be easy to assume that it's in the latter circumstance, when things are not going well, that strategy comes into its own. But that would be to underestimate the power of a good strategy. When times are tough and everything is going pear-shaped, yes, strategy will come to your aid like nothing else. In the bad times, your strategy will behave like a Newfoundland — the big, black, shaggy, bear-like dog which is so famously good at rescuing drowning seamen. **Like a Newfoundland, a good strategy is big, hairy, immensely strong, loyal, patient, intelligent and surprisingly gentle.**

That's in the bad times. But a sound strategy will also be your friend when times are good. Because it's when times are good that you can get carried away by success; or, to quote my wife (because I can often be really guilty of this): "that's when you chase after shiny, pretty things". These shiny, pretty things might be new projects, new opportunities, brand extensions, diversifications and distractions of all kinds. And they might all appear to be not just attractive but also completely rational. If there's one thing all entrepreneurs, and all ideas-driven people are really good at it's rationalizing our behaviour. That's not to say that every new idea or opportunity which comes along is by definition a distraction: but the challenge is telling the shiny/pretty things apart from the real gems. And that is precisely where your big hairy rescue dog called strategy comes in; a good strategy will insistently tug you away from distractions and will guard you against rash decisions.

So we've established why and when we need a strategy, but what makes one set of thoughts a strategy, as opposed to a plan (cunning or otherwise), and what distinguishes a strategy from the concept it is so often associated with: tactics?

This is the simplest and best definition that I know:

Strategy describes where you want to go. In the broadest sense, strategy is a description of your desired outcome. It can be fairly general and 'big picture' or it can be supported by some level of detail. But it's essentially about destination and desirability. Strategy should **not** muddy its own waters by explaining how that desirable destiny or outcome is reached. That's not strategy, that's tactics.The most challenging element of all when creating a strategy is to avoid this confusion with tactics.

Tactics describe how you are going to reach the destination or the outcome. Tactics are descriptions of the things you or your business or a team are actually going to do. Tactics can be fairly detailed, or fairly sketchy. In other words, if you're talking about what you're going to do in the coming week and you're talking about your own actions or that of a very small team, then when you talk tactics you might well be pretty detailed. You might go down to the level of who exactly does what exactly, at what time tomorrow exactly. But tactics can also be more general depending on the timescale involved, numbers of people involved, and the degree to which you are devolving decision-making and accountability.

See the difference? And before we move on, watch out for the somewhat confusing concept of 'strategic planning'. You'll find it out there in management literature and in the documentation within lots of companies. But it's not a helpful concept for us, precisely because it muddies the waters. Planning is about how you get where you're going and predicting some of the things which might happen along the way, and how you might respond to them. Nothing wrong with that, of course, but it isn't strategy.

So keep strategy separate; it's about where you want to go. And that's what we'll look at now, in an analytical (but nonetheless creative) way.

Brand Builder Workout

We're going to work with a technique called Morphological Analysis or MA (don't stop reading, this is fun as well as productive, and nowhere near as complicated as it sounds).

Dr Fritz Zwicky (1898–1974) was a Bulgarian-born, Swiss-raised astrophysicist and aerospace scientist, based for more than 25 years at CalTech (the California Institute of Technology), where he made a huge contribution to the development of modern jet and rocket engines. Zwicky's relevance to us in looking at brand strategy stems from his need to investigate scientific problems which involved elements that could not be easily compared with one another. In other words, scientific problems that did not yield easily to conventional analysis through the lens of the microscope or even through the application of advanced mathematics or physics.

Zwicky created a beautifully simple system for comparing and relating things which are of a different and incomparable nature: apples and walking boots, for example. Or zebras and geography. In other words, it allows you to look at things that aren't much alike and to compare and connect them. Zwicky used his technique to crack fiendishly difficult problems of aerospace engineering, such as which energy sources to use with which propulsion systems. But we can use MA to tackle almost any problem that looks like it can't be solved logically; problems which some of Zwicky's followers referred to as 'wicked' problems.

The actual device that Fritz used to do this is known as a Morphological Box. And that is? Well, it's not really a box for starters: it's more of a grid. You could draw one on a piece of paper very simply, and that's a great way to try it out. In fact, we're not just trying out a technique here, we're creating the basics of a brand strategy: so here goes. Grab a big bit of paper and a pen (or preferably pens of several different colours).

Draw yourself a grid made up of four columns and eight rows, which should give you a total of 32 little boxes. The trick with this technique is to remember the difference between rows and columns. It's easy, as you'll see, but it's also important not to mix them up. The columns are technically known as 'parameters'. We'll call them 'aspects'. I'll explain.

A very simple Morphological Analysis box.

First we need our 'problem', and it's important that we state it very clearly. In fact, stating the problem clearly is the most important step in using this technique. Let's say our problem is that we want to open a new coffee shop (a remarkably common business idea) but we're not sure what kind of coffee shop might be the most successful. We're using the term 'coffee shop' to embrace anything in that general field (tea shop, café, milk bar, etc.) but for our purposes it isn't going to include wine bar or pub.

Now we need to stick a header on each column, representing a different 'aspect' of our coffee shop idea. Let's say column 1 is going to be 'location' (which is obviously concerned with where your coffee shop will be), so scribble 'location' above Column 1. Likewise, Column 2 can be 'style', column 3 can be 'customer type', and finally column 4 can be 'business emphasis'.

I've picked these just to suit the example, of course. When you use this on your own business you'll almost certainly need more columns, but these will do to illustrate the method.

Now shift your attention to the rows. Under each column heading you've got space for eight possible variables. So under 'location', for example, you've got space to note up to eight different possible locations for our imaginary coffee shop. In my example I've put:

- mall
- city precinct
- business district
- side street
- mobile van
- college campus
- village
- seaside

The same principle applies to the other columns. Note that in my example, one of the columns only has seven possibilities listed: there is no right number. You might not fill every row, or you can add more rows if you think of more possibilities.

Location	Style	Business emphasis	Possible customers
Mall	Italian	Grab & Go	Shoppers
City precinct	American diner	Relax and have another	Office workers
Business district	English teashoppe	Gourmet coffee	Commuters
Side street	Minimalist	Home made food	Students
Mobile van	African	Deliveries	Families
College Campus	Mod	Pay for time not coffee	Children and Mums
Village	Child-oriented	Fairtrade	Tourists
Seaside		Organic	OAPs

Just 4096 permutations for a coffee shop brand!

You should now have 32 boxes, each with a word or phrase in it. Here's the science bit (as they say in the shampoo commercials): the elements of one column are not really comparable with the elements in another. 'Mall', for example, is not really a term that's easily analyzed next to, or compared with 'home-made food'. Mall and home-made food are, in effect, our new zebras and geography. Things of a different nature. But the Morphological

Box allows us to look at them all with equal clarity, in a non-hierarchical way. This is what makes it such a powerful creative technique, because hierarchies of ideas are the enemy of creative thinking and absolutely not what we want at this stage of creating our brand strategy.

Studying this Morphological Box for just a few minutes will reveal a host of possibilities that would in all probability not have occurred to you just by sitting and thinking about the coffee shop challenge as a whole. And this happens because you can join up any variable in column 1 with any other in columns 2, 3 and 4. If you do the maths you'll see that even a relatively small Morphological Box like this one will give you lots of different possible coffee shop models. In fact, if you haven't come across this approach before you may not guess at first that even this simple little grid of four columns and eight rows gives you an astonishing (well I was astonished anyway) 4096 different coffee shop ideas. The maths is simple once you know: in our case it's just $8 \times 8 \times 8 \times 8 = 4096$.

Not enough possibilities for you? Add another column with another header, say 'pricing', and dream up another eight possibilities under that header (which could include cheap, premium, offer-based, etc.) and you will have increased the overall permutations to a staggering 32,768.

And that is the absolute beauty of this approach to beginning your brand strategy. Not even a fully qualified marketing genius is going to be able to dream up 32,768 different kinds of coffee shop business through conventional thinking. And I promise you that no amount of 'brainstorming' with your team will be as productive.

Add just one more row of variables to your five columns and you'll have a (possibly unnecessary) 59,049 possibilities. And, of course, you can join up variables within the same column (so the same shop could be aimed at business people and commuters, perhaps at different times of day), which multiplies your creative options still further.

Once you've got your Morphological Box populated with different variables under different headings (which, by the way, is known as a morphological field), what next? Well, this technique helps the would-be entrepreneur and brand-builder in a host of ways. We'll look at some of them now.

Great benefit number one of this approach is that it removes all the anxiety and tension from creating a new business idea. That's simply because it does not ask you to be 'creative' when you start. Often, the scariest thing about trying to think creatively about a business or a brand is just knowing where to start. Thanks to Fritz Zwicky, as long as you can state your question clearly, the Morphological Box will do the starting-up for you. It's like a marvellous creative-thinking machine that you can control. In fact, the technique works most effectively when you fill the boxes with random possibilities that occur to you, rather than trying to be creative in the normal sense. When a column heading says 'customers', your best bet is just to write down the first eight types of customer you can think of.

The second great benefit is that the box will throw up possible brand and business ideas that you wouldn't otherwise have thought of. You might have woken up in the middle of the night with the brainwave of opening a coffee shop which served really great gourmet coffee, but would you have considered the possibility that it might be a real hit if it was mobile and could visit your local college campus in the morning and several nearby villages in the afternoons?

Your dream might be to open a café in your favourite seaside town. Well, you can probably rule out commuters and students as your key customer groups. But you might well choose to concentrate on giving tourists an exceptional coffee experience, or on serving the needs of local pensioners (or both).

Morphological Analysis also has the great virtue (although it is, by definition, highly analytical) of linking directly back to our last chapter and therefore to your emotional ambitions and desires. Imagine, for example, that you're Italian. It might be (though not necessarily, of course) a key part of your coffee-shop ambition to bring to life Italian coffee shop 'values' and spirit. If this is the case then you might want to begin your path-making across the grid at 'Italian' under the style heading. From that point you can move in any direction, and certain things on the grid will seem like a natural fit, whilst others will not. On the other hand, you might have a deep-rooted enthusiasm for certain aspects of 1960s' culture, and therefore want to start with 'Mod' and move out from there. Or you might be a fierce advocate of all things Fairtrade and so start there, and so on.

Depending on your circumstances you might start not with your emotions or imagination, but with practical needs. Perhaps our ideal is to be on the

High Street, but rents make it unaffordable whilst a short-term tenancy is available for a café on a business park. There is no single right place to start because the grid, as we've said before, is anti-hierarchical.

Using the Morphological box you can quickly generate a number of different possibilities around the broad theme of coffee shop, or whatever your key business idea is. It's really a matter of drawing pathways across the grid (partly why I recommend using different coloured pens). You can see in the final example some of the possibilities that might be worth exploring if this coffee shop idea was your business.

Location	Style	Business emphasis	Possible customers
Mall	Italian	Grab & Go	Shoppers
City precinct	American diner	Relax and have another	Office workers
Business district	English teashoppe	Gourmet coffee	Commuters
Side street	Minimalist	Home made food	Students
Mobile van	African	Deliveries	Families
College Campus	Mod	Pay for time not coffee	Children and Mums
Village	Child-oriented	Fairtrade	Tourists
Seaside		Organic	OAPs

Here's just two of the possibilities highlighted.

Once you've got your possible routes you can choose to go forward with one, two, three or more to the next stages of your brand development. Remember, whatever grid you've created, no matter how messy it might appear once you've drawn numerous pathways across it, keep it somewhere safe. Just like your letter from the future, your grid is part of your essential brand research, and it's yet another reason why your brand is more likely to succeed than one which hasn't been explored as yours has been.

REAL BRAND STORY

BPHA

David Keeling, Executive Director for Development and Property at bpha (Bedfordshire Pilgrims Housing Association) explains how the organization used clear brand strategy to win a national housing competition.

The Cambridge Challenge competition proposed a radical change to the creation of new homes and communities by using one partner to deliver all the affordable housing in a huge development programme based around the city of Cambridge.

For the [then] Housing Corporation, the competition tested whether identifying a single development partner could maximize the impact of its grant fund. For the winner, it offered an exceptional opportunity to develop 3300 affordable homes on the sites.

We put together a consortium of housing associations — which we named 'Cambridgeshire Partnerships' — that we believed offered the right mix of development experience and specialist housing expertise to deliver the schemes and together we entered the fray.

We weren't the biggest player in the Cambridge Challenge and we weren't the most powerful so we had the biggest hurdles to overcome. But we knew that we had what it took to deliver this extraordinary project and we absolutely believed we would do it better than anyone else.

In many respects, this formed the basis of our brand strategy. We believed that the way to win was to convey a sense of what we were about and what we could offer. This had to be attractive to the stakeholders we needed to influence and, ultimately, the decision makers.

We developed a number of key themes that defined our bid: strength, professionalism, knowledge, a good partner with whom to do business, innovation, trust and local commitment. Local commitment was particularly important to us – our research told us it would be key to our success but it also fitted in well with our corporate aims.

Alongside working out what we wanted to say, we also undertook a major analysis of our competitors' offers, which gave us information about what we needed to do to make our offer stand out.

We then set about conveying our themes using a multifaceted approach.

Firstly, we made a lot of background noise. We made sure we were mentioned everywhere! I almost became a regular on Radio Cambridgeshire and BBC Look East at one point but the important thing was to get our name mentioned positively, in many places and frequently.

Then we made sure that we targeted our messages specifically at the right people. In this competition the major players had varied and sometimes conflicting interests. We researched what was important to these players and then worked individually with them all to build confidence in us, so although we remained true to our principles, we also made sure we emphasized different elements of our offer to the different parties.

Crucially, in remaining true to our principles we not only said what we stood for, we made sure that what we did was consistent with that — we stuck to one of our Chief Executive's favourite phrases 'we do what we say'.

And finally, we encapsulated what we were about with the development of the look and feel for our partnership. It was essential to get this right. It was the visual representation of everything we stood for. Having heard Simon Middleton talk about brand strategy I thought he was the right person to advise us and we brought him in.

Keen to underline our local commitment, we asked Simon to mock up logo options with a Cambridgeshire theme. Discarding overexposed images like Kings College Chapel, Simon's design team took the inspiration for our logo from the pasque flower, Cambridgeshire's county flower. This enabled us to emphasize our local credentials by committing to plant pasque flowers in the proposed Country Park on the largest of the sites. Our strapline 'thriving new communities' emphasized that we were about more than building houses.

All of what we had done and learned along the way was brought together in our final presentation, which I led. We knew we needed to take things to the next level with this — everything rested on it — so we brought Simon back to help us again.

His key advice at this stage was essentially to keep it simple. One speaker, a focused presentation, use of technology that kept the attention on the presentation instead of the faffing of changing slides.

It's history now, we won. There is no doubt in my mind that brand strategy played a key role in our success because our actions created a belief within the minds of the decision makers that Cambridgeshire Partnerships was the right choice to deliver the Cambridge Challenge.

Day 6

TALENT: RECOGNIZING IT AND DEVELOPING IT

Talent's a funny thing. We seem to woefully underestimate it or dangerously overestimate it. I think too many potentially successful business-owners are put off making the big leap to running their own show by a lack of understanding of and conviction in their own talent. Perhaps others dive in with rather too much self-assurance compared to their actual degree of ability. So if you're going to create a brand-oriented business, particularly if you're starting from scratch, then you need to assess and recognize your talent (and the talents of your team) in a realistic way. Only by doing this can you be sure of your strengths and weaknesses.

Most skills involved in running a business can be put into one of two categories.

Category 1 Something you are already skilled at, or something you can learn to do yourself, and learn to do it cost-effectively enough to make it appropriate for you to be spending time doing it.

Category 2 Something that you'll either find deeply challenging or even nigh impossible to learn to do well, or that will take you such a chunk of time to learn and to continue to do that you'd be much better off paying someone else to do it for you.

Which functions fall into each of these categories will vary from person to person and business to business. I decided, by way of example, that I was not only unqualified but distinctly lacking in talent in anything to do with finances/bookkeeping/accounts/taxation. An absolute case of Category 2. Solution? Simple. Find a good accountant to do everything except my invoicing. Sure it costs me money every month to have an accountancy firm do this, but I sleep soundly in my bed and don't get harassed by Her Majesty's Revenue & Customs. And if my business was larger then one of my first appointments would be a qualified and experienced Finance Director.

By contrast, you might be brilliant with money and find all the bookkeeping and accountancy stuff not just a doddle but an absolute pleasure. That's fine. Stick it in Category 1 as something that you'll take care of.

I happen to be comfortable with words, and I've been writing in one way or another for my whole life. So I wouldn't dream of letting anyone else write my media releases, or my blog, or my website. That's a Cat 1 skill for me. But you might not feel skilled and at ease with writing. So don't struggle with it. Don't. For you it's Cat 2. Find a freelance copywriter to do all that for you. There'll be one in your town. Check out a few. A lot of them are really good, and they're nowhere near as expensive as wasting hours trying to do yourself something which isn't you. Funnily enough, even though I love to write, and I think I'm best placed to write about the subject area in which I am working (i.e. branding) I have recently hired a very good freelancer to write the news stories for my monthly newsletter because of my growing workload, and because she researches and writes the stories more quickly and cost-effectively than I would be able to do. There was bit of an emotional hurdle to get over in giving up a task which was so clearly Category 1 for me; but sometimes you just have to look at the bigger picture.

Brand Builder Workout

Here's a list of practical skill-sets which most people would agree are required in running even a small business. Note that these are not business/brand-specific but general. We'll come to the specifics of your business shortly.

- Strategic skills (direction and major decision-making in your business)
- Leadership skills (closely related to strategic skills but more concerned with the ability to motivate people and to take them with you on your journey)

- Branding and marketing skills (the area that this book covers)
- Financial skills (including bookkeeping, accountancy, profit/loss, taxation)
- Legal skills (from employment law to health & safety, food hygiene, intellectual property, licences, etc.)
- Operational management skills (including getting stuff done, from production to distribution, purchasing stock, packaging, etc.)
- Human Resource skills (hiring, training and looking after your people)
- Sales skills (depending on what kind of business you run)
- Computer skills (including office networks, website creation, databases)

Which of these would you put in Category 1 (you can do them yourself, comfortably) and which in Category 2 (you need to get someone else to do them)?

To answer the question accurately you might have to explore a few of these skill-sets in a bit more detail than we have room for here. You might, for example, be very experienced in hiring new staff (perhaps in a previous job in a larger organization). So you might be tempted to put Human Resource skills in Category 1. But explore it a little more first. Are you up-to-date with employment law, with training requirements and so on? Maybe you will need help after all. Maybe it's Category 2.

If you do this exercise thoroughly you'll be in a very good position to decide what help you need: what other talent you need around you. But don't jump to the conclusion that you need to hire full time people to fill these skill gaps. Most skill-sets can be hired on a freelance or part-time or temporary basis. My advice to all small businesses and nascent brands is to hire in help when you need it, rather than committing to permanent employment of people until you absolutely need it. Remember this book is about building a brand in 30 days, not building a multi-person organization just for the sake of it.

So much for the 'general' skills involved in running a business. None of them, I would argue, are beyond you: either to do yourself or to do effectively if you get the right help. But what about the more interesting stuff: the skills and talents that are distinctive and 'core' to you, and might become so to your brand and your business? I have to return to my earlier point that some of us underestimate our skills whilst others of us wildly exaggerate our gifts. Neither error is going to help us: we need to be accurate enough to be confident. That's all.

Using my business as an example again. My background is in advertizing, on the creative side in the main (dreaming up and writing ads). But I also found myself running workshops about branding and creativity for clients. And I have some teaching history. And a bit of National Health Service experience to give me knowledge of communication and management inside a really large organization. It didn't take long to work out that I had the appropriate skills and the beginnings of the know-how applicable to developing a specialized brand-strategy advisory business. In other words, my business idea grew out of three key roots:

1. *Proven talents*   (writing, idea generation, communication);

2. *Real passions/interests*   (writing, problem-solving, teaching others);

3. *Evidence of a market*   (heaps of evidence during my years in advertizing that people were hungry to learn about branding and to learn its essential skills).

That's not to say that I didn't have lots more to learn, even in my chosen area. Before I left my agency job to set up on my own I had only really scratched the surface of the required in-depth branding knowledge. There was plenty of work to do, and I have to continue to work hard to keep up. You'll never get away from that. But these three roots gave me the well-founded self-confidence to make the jump.

Brand Builder Workout

Try the exercise for yourself. Answer the questions honestly and fully. If there is a deep connection between your answers to each question then I think you are in good shape. If there is a gulf between, say, your proven talents and your real passions/interests then you have a challenge, which we will come back to in a moment.

1. *Write down your 'proven talents': the things you know you're good at and/or very knowledgeable about, and which you have proved to yourself and others that you're good at.* (By the way, you don't have to be 'gifted'. Just 'good'. You know the difference. If in doubt at all, in fact I recommend you do this anyway, ask some people who know you well to validate your answers. You may have left something out. Don't be shy.)

2. *Write down your 'real passions/interests'.* Don't make value judgements yet about whether they are important. Don't dismiss anything. Just list the things that really turn you on.

Take a pause here and compare items under 1 and 2. Is there any commonality? Is there an obvious connection? If there is you are fortunate indeed, as was I when I started out. Maybe this is where your business/brand future lies. If there is no connection at all then don't panic: you still have three very positive options.

A. You can take one of your passions and explore it further. Is there a skill related to that passion which you can learn/develop?

B. You can concentrate on the skills area. It's perfectly possible to develop the passion later. And frequently the passion will come from the challenge of running the business itself and in developing the brand.

C. You can put passions and skills to one side for a moment and focus on the next question 'evidence of a market' (and this is a perfectly good route, depending on your personality).

3. *Write down the 'evidence of a market'.* This is the toughie. Just because you are highly skilled at assembling, maintaining, repairing and modifying bicycles and you are also a passionate cyclist doesn't necessarily mean there is is a market for a business based on this. There might be. But you don't know that yet.

I don't mean you need to carry out a massive research project. But I do mean not diving into business naively. In a few chapters' time we will look into this in more detail, under the heading of context.

///

To summarize, these three big questions make a kind of triangle, as I've drawn here.

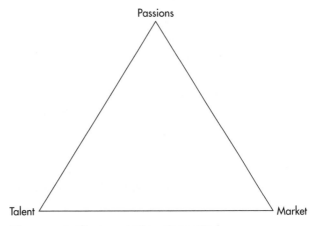

Three mutually supporting elements.

All three elements (talent, passions, market) are connected and, to one degree or another, interdependent. But my rule of thumb is that you don't need all three to be fully resolved when you start out. Trying to put everything in place can paralyze you. And this is where, as a 'brand' person rather than a 'marketing' person, I take a different view from most people giving advice to new businesses.

Many such advisors and commentators would argue that 'evidence of a market' is the most important factor here: and that unless there is clear evidence of an existing demand for your product or your service then you would be reckless to begin. I don't agree. One thing is certain in business and that is that nobody really has any idea what will succeed or not. Markets can spring up out of nowhere just as products can. Who would have thought in the mid-1970s that there would be a market for a cassette tape recorder that you carried around on your belt, still less one that didn't actually record anything? Yet in 1979 the Sony Walkman appeared and everything changed. Thirty years later our entire music industry has changed. Our entire attitude to popular music has changed. Sure that's got a lot to do with technological developments. But it's also got a great deal to do with a small group of maverick product developers in Sony, working (as legend has it) against the explicit instructions of their bosses.

So my suggestion is this: if you can be positive about any two corners of the triangle you could be onto something. All three corners and you could be really off to a flying start.

But don't forget the first half of this chapter: **don't try to do everything yourself. Play to your talents**.

Day 7

Establishing Your Brand Values (the Things You Won't Compromise)

The best brands in the world are built on distinctive but very solid values, sometimes a set of them, sometimes just one. Volvo is built entirely on the value of 'safety': precisely the value it started with nearly a century ago. This chapter will help you to create a set of values that is robust, distinctive, long-lasting and powerful.

Hang on a minute though. Haven't values been a bit discredited? Aren't they just meaningless statements that get stuck on posters on the wall or hung from banners in large offices, or printed on little cards for your wallet? Values in business have certainly been vulnerable to misuse, misunderstanding and thus to a negative reputation. But actually, when you think about it, apart from our biologically hard-wired instincts, values are really all we humans have got to guide our decisions and our behaviour. Values are pretty fundamental. And if they're fundamental to people then they should be fundamental to business, and to brands.

Brand by our definition is about meaning: and **nothing generates and supports meaning like values**. So this chapter is about urging you to explore, examine, clarify and express the values that will underwrite your brand. But how on earth do you choose a set of values?

Remember that what you're always looking for in branding is a beautiful combination of distinctiveness, authenticity and compelling story. Those three elements give us the clue to establishing and using values. It's enormously tempting when we speak of values in business to grab at two kinds of values, and many brand owners fall into a trap this way.

The first type of value we tend to reach for might be called the 'too broad, too obvious' values. Values like honesty, fairness, support, teamwork, innovation, or even friendliness or customer-focused.

There is nothing wrong with these as concepts. We all want to be fair and supportive, to be good team members, to be innovative and so on. But that's precisely the problem with these concepts as guiding values. They're just too bland and ordinary. They all beg the question: 'as opposed to what exactly?' Take fairness as a value as opposed to dishonesty. Oh, that's all right then, all your customers will be hugely relieved and reassured that you aren't going to behave dishonestly, because honesty is one of your values. And they'll come flooding through your door because you're committed to teamwork as opposed to your every-man-for-himself competitor. See what I mean? **Bland values are as worthless as no values at all**.

The second type of value that many businesses put in the values grab bag are those that I think of as 'the big swaggering, and probably unachievable' values. These aren't quite so easy to spot as the too broad and too obvious ones, but they are just as important to watch out for and to avoid. They often have superlatives attached to them: best practice (...in whatever field you care to mention); market leading (...something or other); best in class (which always sounds like one's in a dog show); and one of my absolute favourite meaningless values, world class.

It's not that I want to limit anybody's ambitions. Quite the opposite. But really, you can't make world class one of your values because it just isn't one. It's an aspiration, and not a very helpful one at that. So how do you establish your brand's values, and is it worth all the fuss? It definitely is worth the fuss and the effort because your brand values will not only act as a compass and a constant reference for your brand's behaviour and development as you move forward, but they will also provide a strong anchor for your customers' relationship with the brand. And actually it's not that difficult to do as this exercise will show.

Brand Builder Workout

I recommend that you start with a grid method, not unlike the Fritz Zwicky Morphological Analysis grid that you used in the last chapter on brand strategy. This time, though, the grid is simpler and easier, because it doesn't need to be arranged in columns with headers. All you have to do is draw a simple grid like the one shown below. I recommend a pretty large grid with lots of boxes to accommodate all your potential values (because that's what we're about to fill it with). Maybe 8 × 8, which will give you 64 squares.

The values grid. Draw it large!

The next bit is simple and fun. Either working alone, or with your team, write just one value that you'd like to consider for your brand in each box. It's fine if at this stage you enter all kinds of value concepts (including the broad-bland ones and the swaggering-unachievable ones), because we're going to interrogate them and edit them at the next stage. After a bit of head scratching and hard work you should have a grid populated with all kinds of values concepts.

When you are filling in the grid, remind yourself and your team what we mean by a value: a concept or a principle that seems important enough to guide your behaviour and your decision-making. A value should be something to live by. A value can be very specific or it can be fairly broad-based.

And a quick tip: when you are completing the grid try to enter the values randomly across it. Start in the middle perhaps, and put the next one somewhere far away on one side or in the corner. Put the next one somewhere else. This is important because we're not making an hierarchy at this point. The whole point of the grid is that it is a catch-all. It doesn't give any more importance to any one idea over any other.

Once your grid is full, or as full as you can happily make it without straining your brain and resorting to sticking in values you don't really believe in (you'll know when you've reached that stage), it's time for the interrogation. Now to do this properly requires some tough and objective thinking. You're going to take each value in turn and focus on it, and ask some very tough questions. Here they come.

1. ***Is this value genuine?*** Do you actually, honestly, believe that this is important to you and your brand? If the answer is YES keep it in the mix. If NO then it's fallen at the first hurdle. Strike it out. No second chances (ruthlessness is one of my values, when it comes to assessing values).

2. ***Is this value liveable?*** Do you really, truly think that your brand and business (and therefore by definition your people) can actually live by this value? YES: keep it in the frame. NO: dump it, because a value that you can't actually live by is no value at all.

3. *Is this value compelling internally?*   Does it have emotional as well as intellectual power: the power to engage and motivate your people? Has it got the potential to affect positively the way they work, behave and even think about the brand and their role in it? Usual routine. YES means it stays in the mix for now. NO puts it out of the running.

4. *Will this value mean anything to your customers?*   Will anybody care? Honestly: if your customers or prospects learn about this value, will it make them more likely to do business with you? Does it tap into their concerns and interests? YES? Good, it's still in with a chance. NO? It's out. Because values have to mean something to customers too, otherwise, what's the point?

5. *Is this value 'relevant' to your brand?*   Does this value have some resonance with the actual content and meaning of your brand and business? If you import coffee or sell furniture then values connected to fair trade or renewable resources are relevant, of course. But if you're a bicycle repair shop then a slavish adherence to British-sourced parts is going to limit your business more than a little.

A quick note at this point. You might be feeling, if you've been as ruthless as I suggest, that you're going to end up with a very small set of values. But don't panic: few is good for a host of reasons. A few values mean they will have survived all these tough questions and will therefore be more powerful and meaningful as a result. And having just a few values (or even just one, like Volvo) will massively increase your chances of educating your people and your customers about what you stand for and stand by. Few is good.

6. *Does this value contribute to you being distinctive as a brand?*   This one is probably best explained through example. Let's say you're a pork pie maker (I happen to know one). If one of your values is that the meat in your pies is always and only the same kind of meat you'd find in chops and joints (i.e. the good stuff), then you are in the happy position of having a brand value that actually contributes to your brand distinctiveness. Because there will be few others who will claim this. Note, it doesn't have to be 'unique' (nothing is unique) but it does have to be 'unusual'. And notice the specific nature of this brand value. Therein lies its power. YES to distinctive? Keep it in the list. NO to distinctive? Out it goes. This question is a killer for the bland values. Quality is often put forward as a value, for example, and it always falls at this fence.

7. ***Does this value have longevity/sustainability?* Values, like puppies, should be for life, not just for Christmas.** Ask yourself if you can picture this value still being pertinent and powerful a year from now. Five years from now. Twenty years from now. YES and it stays in. NO and it's out.

8. ***Can you communicate this value to people?*** Can you explain it, justify it, enthuse about it? Does it make sense? Is it clear enough to grasp? Could you and anyone in your team instantly recall it and explain it to a customer, to a visitor, to a journalist? YES? That's magic. NO? Dump it or refine it. There might be something in it, but you're going to have to craft it because a value that too vague or difficult to explain just isn't going to be very helpful.

9. ***Can this value be brought to life in behaviour?*** A value that doesn't result in behaviour change isn't really worth its salt. Can this value be made real by what you and your people actually do in terms of service, or product design, or the customer experience, or quality of what you deliver? If the answer is YES then it could be a winner. If the answer is NO then it's unlikely to ever be anything other than an empty promise, and empty promises are not worth making.

10. ***Would you fight to preserve this value?*** To put it bluntly, is this a value in which you believe so strongly that you simply will not compromise it? Is it core to your personal belief system? Is it fundamental to why you created this brand in the first place? If you can't wait to say YES to this one, be careful here... there's danger in this question as well as power! It's good to believe in something passionately, but watch out for those personal convictions that are so strong they will get in the way of the brand. You might have a very strong religious conviction, for example, and if you do then that will indeed guide your life and your behaviour; but you must also ask yourself if it should really govern your brand. Questions 1 to 8 will help you decide. On the other hand, if you answer NO then, as per the other questions, you have to leave this off your list. Only you can decide on the right balance with this question.

//

They were 10 tough questions: have any of your values survived? If a few have, then it's highly likely that they are going to be genuinely powerful and useful to you. If none got through, then I'd suggest a re-examination of your original list. Maybe, now that you've taken your first thoughts through the test a few more will spring to mind which can really survive and help to shape your brand.

And now, whether you've got a clutch of half a dozen values or even just one or two, you are well on the way. But they may still need crafting to make them memorable and useful in everyday life. I suggest a simple method for doing this.

Step 1: give your value a short and memorable name   For example in our pork pie example we might name that value 'the good stuff'.

Step 2: give your value a succinct explanation   For example: "Our pork pies are always and only made with the meat you'd find in chops and joints."

Step 3: describe how your value is brought to life in practical terms   This might actually be a list of 'rules'. But keep it short and positive. It's not meant to be a lecture, just to make sure there's no doubt about what this value means.

The final thing to remember about values as the basis of your brand is that once you declare your values you must live by them in everything you do. If your value is 'hand-made...' then you'd better not be found mass producing. **Values are powerful things indeed: but they have a way of punishing those who misuse them** just as they will reward those who live by them.

REAL BRAND STORY

Adnams

Andy Wood, Managing Director of Adnams plc, explains how the traditional brewer built a powerful and sustainable brand in a declining market by focusing on its values.

In many people's eyes, Adnams is a very traditional business and in one sense that is absolutely so, underpinned by the fact that Adnams has been brewing traditional beer and owning pubs and hotels in and around its home in Southwold, Suffolk since 1872.

Today, however, Adnams is a vibrant modern business that sells its wares both nationally and internationally. We have a turnover of approximately £50m and employ around 350 people. In our recent history we have reinvented ourselves around what we describe as a 'values based' business model. In lay terms, that means being very clear about what we stand for — our values — being very clear about the contribution we require from leaders and staff and being very clear that we have many stakeholders beyond the traditional definitions of shareholders, staff and customers. Adnams today has built a broad coalition between business and community and within its heartland is viewed as a much-loved brand. This enviable position has been achieved through the recognition that the brand is a living, breathing thing that is an amalgam of our external face, our logo, the way we behave and the way we engage our people to deliver for the customer. The recognition of these simple concepts has seen our business develop a desirable reputation and high levels of brand recognition amongst our target customers. This position has seen us consistently outperform our chosen markets over a sustained period of around ten years and develop an international reputation for our work in the field of sustainable business practice.

How has this all been achieved?

1. Around 1999/2000 we defined our core values. These were to be the framework for the way in which we were going to operate for the foreseeable future. In themselves the values were not particularly distinctive and contained similar words that would be readily found in any other businesses statement of values. But it was not the values themselves that would set the business apart but the way in which they were implemented.

2. The top team consulted widely on defining the values and fully immersed themselves in making them more than just words on a page. They committed fully to bringing them to life in real and tangible ways. This involved behavioural change throughout the organization and an understanding that the business was committing to long term and fundamental change that would not be easy to unwind if people didn't like it or felt uncomfortable.

3. The team committed to realizing the full creative power of its employees, through rewarding ideas, allowing people to take risks and being unswerving in its support of the notion of 'catching people doing things right'.

4. The team committed to investment decisions that would not only meet traditional financial cost-benefit analysis requirements but also reflect espoused values.

5. We also realized that effective implementation of the plan required a strong understanding and working partnership with suppliers. We set out to work with the very best people we could afford.

6. Reputation was the fundamental pillar upon which a values-based business was going to rest and so we started to engage more fully in our local communities building upon a long-standing history of charitable giving. We encouraged staff at all levels to get involved, to take part and to do the right thing. This approach extended into facing up to the difficulties that can be caused by excess alcohol consumption. In this field we took a bold leadership position around education, working with young people, working with charities and being one of the first producers to implement unit and foetal alcohol syndrome labelling on its packaging. A counter-intuitive position to most of our industry peers at the time.

Finally, our business had to understand and define the core proposition to its customers. The outward-facing component parts of the Adnams brand are conviviality, sociability, relaxation, refreshment and quality of life allied to a not-too-serious demeanour. From these components a brand truth was developed, and encapsulated in the award-winning 'Beer from the Coast' campaign. This work communicates so vividly that — *Ah! That's better* — moment for our customers.

And the impact? Since the late 1990s we have managed to almost double output and grow share in a market that has been in long-term and significant decline. We have managed to sustain dividends for shareholders whilst investing heavily in renewing core infrastructure. We have implemented state-of-the-art technologies in brewing and in our award-winning distribution centre.

We achieve high levels of customer acquisition and retention and fantastic levels of staff engagement, with over 90% of staff being either proud or very proud to work here. We have received the Queen's Award for sustainable development, the Carbon Trust's Carbon Innovator of the Year award and the Business in the Community eco efficiency award. In 2007 we brought to market the UK's first carbon-neutral beer which transformed our relationship with some of the UK's largest retailers and sees us now positioned as one of the most innovative companies in the UK brewing sector. Our pubs and hotels continue to thrive and our new Adnams Cellar & Kitchen retail concept, (created following brand research that suggested the brand was overtly masculine), continues to make strong progress balancing any gender bias and attracting new and younger customers to the brand.

Day 8

Putting Your Brand in Context: Finding Out What's Out There

Creating a winning brand is, at least in part, dependent on understanding your competition and then out-flanking it, not by spending more money, but by being more distinctive, more compelling and more emotionally engaging. And you don't need to hire an agency to analyze your market place. This chapter shows you how to do it fast, thoroughly and effectively.

First of all you need to define **who** your competitors are. Your competition comes in two broad types:

1. Businesses that are quite like yours in terms of their products and services. In other words **competing in what they do**.

2. Businesses that offer different products and services to yours but which are aimed at similar people, because of either location or niche interest (say, 'cyclists' or 'cooks'). In other words **competing in who they sell to**.

Brand Builder Workout

So to begin with, try this simple exercise, starting with Category 1. Just write down as a simple list all the businesses you can think of that fall into this category: everyone who offers a similar product or service to you. To make it easier, try putting these competitors under three headings:

A. Local competitors (that is, businesses in your locality).

B. National competitors (businesses who operate on a national scale but who can compete with you online or through media advertising and so on).

C. International competitors (remember, you might be a highly distinctive local food producer but you still have to compete with international food brands in supermarkets).

Now it's time to look at each of the competitors on your lists in a little more detail. As you look at each business name you need to answer four (sort of simple) questions, as follows. Actually it isn't the questions that are difficult, but the answers. Or at least answering honestly.

1. In what ways is this competitor better than you? Think about their pricing, their reputation, their style, their attitude, their customer service, their choice, their quality and so on. Don't pull your punches here: it's important to really get the measure of these guys!

2. In what ways can you deliver a brand experience which trumps theirs? Can you provide better quality products, better service, more choice, more specialized advice, a deeper selection of products albeit across a narrower range? Can you make buying from you a pleasure instead of a chore, and if so how?

3. What do you think the brand of this competitor 'stands for'? What does it mean? Are they primarily about price, or choice, or expertise, or service or something else?

4. What are you going to 'stand for' that is different from them?

It's straightforward as a process, but you might be reluctant to work through these questions with a list of 10 or more competitors. Please don't be put off. Each time you go through these questions about a competitor you will be one step closer to honing a brand for your business or organization which is distinct and compelling, even in apparently crowded market places.

You'd think, wouldn't you, that there are enough coffee shops in the world? Yet they continue to open on every high street and side street in every town. Those that survive and thrive are those which have created a distinctive brand experience. **Don't be frightened by the competition: but do get the measure of it**.

Of course there is one very practical additional step that you can take to assess the competition still further, and I thoroughly recommend it. Become a customer of your competitors and assess them directly from the point of view of the customer. Add this direct experience to your assessment using the questions above.

In the end, of course, only you can decide whether you think you stand a chance of out-flanking the competition. Just remember that it's not a matter of how big your business is, or how much money you spend. It's a matter of brand behaviour and you might be better placed to behave like a great brand than many apparently stronger competitors.

One final word on competition. If you think that you have no competitors at all, be very, very cautious. If you are doing something so different that no-one else appears to be doing it all, there might be a very good reason.

Day 9 and 10

Use Your Imagination

The big corporates often forget that we are creatures of emotion, passion and soul, not just buying machines. By contrast, brilliant brands use metaphor, imagination and even myth to engage our human spirit. It takes courage, not money, to use the power of imagination in your brand. In this chapter, I want to encourage you to let go of fact and process and 'being sensible' for a while to explore the imaginative side of brand.

Byfords in Holt, Norfolk in the UK is part café, part restaurant, part 'posh' B&B. But what do they call it on their website? They call it 'a higgledy piggledy world of pleasure'. In that one simple example you have the essence of the use of imagination in brand. It's a descriptor that speaks directly to our emotions and to our souls, to the child within us.

Of course Byfords can only make this wonderful claim because it lives up to the promise. It is indeed a higgledy piggledy world of pleasure. In part that's because of the wonderful ancient building which it occupies. But only in small part, actually. The real magic of the place is what Iain and his wife and his team have brought to it.

In their vision it's not enough to provide a good café. They want to provide an experience which people will talk about. They want to make an experience that goes way beyond a good product or a good service; one which speaks to our souls.

I hope you don't think I've gone soft here. Far from it. The soulful approach to the concept of the teashop means Byfords is an extraordinary brand success. Strong evidence that the approach works are the 7000 customers a week . It doesn't just work, it leaves all competition in the dust.

And if there were any need to prove the point, Byfords' owners have taken precisely the same approach with a village pub not far away and turned it into a destination gastro-pub that retains an amazing village-pub atmosphere whilst attracting diners from all over Norfolk. And they've repeated the trick with a failing market-town pub which they have reinvented to become a modern take on a classic small-town boozer. All three businesses are thriving. It's a remarkable achievement and it's due to the fact that the owners, like all natural brand geniuses, think and plan in a way that is deeply in touch with human emotion and imagination.

It's an approach that you just can't fake. Thankfully though, it is one that you can learn.

For many people starting new businesses, matters of the heart, soul and imagination take a poor secondary position (if they have a po-sition at all) when compared to practical issues like business plans, bank loans, premises and so on. It's completely understandable, but it's highly regrettable. I'm convinced that if more entrepreneurs spent more 'quality time' with their imaginations then their brands would be stronger, more distinctive and more compelling.

And when I say imagination, I don't mean going all zany! I mean tapping into the truth that we humans are creatures of emotion and imagination.

Let me give you a few examples before we move on to some sugges-tions. Are you a First Direct customer? If not, try this simple quiz.

Q. What happens when you phone First Direct?

A. Somebody answers the phone.

Why is this interesting? Because First Direct have made themselves exceptional through the simple understanding that, beyond any other transactional requirement, what we really want to do when we phone our bank, or any other organization, is **to talk to someone**! So this bank has put substantial resources at the front end of their business. You might describe this as simple customer service, but that would be to miss the point. It's not just customer service; it's an effort of imagination and empathy on the part of a bank. That's exceptional. That's brand. Take a few examples from the world of motoring. Why was the New Mini such a runaway success for BMW? Because it tapped into the powerful emotion of nostalgia. The New Mini shamelessly mimics the original 1960s Mini designed by Issigonis. It's bigger and bulkier, of course — modern cars always are compared to their counterparts from previous generations, largely because they contain contemporary necessities like crumple zones. And if you put a New Mini next to an old one it's not exactly a facsimile. It still retains much of the old car's impracticality, of course, but that doesn't matter, in fact that's part of the point. Because this is a car designed to press emotional buttons. With arguably less success VW's new Beetle was doing the same thing. And at the time of writing the latest love-bug to make a powerful emotional connection with a large motoring audience is the Fiat 500, a car which literally makes people say "aahhh" as if it were a cute kitten.

Now you might say these three vehicles are just trading on the power of nostalgia. But that's only partly true. There are plenty of other cars from the past that could be mimicked today and which would in all probability have no emotional resonance at all. A new take on the Austin Allegro anyone?

No, the reason the Fiat 500 is making such an impact is not just nostalgia. It's because it has succeeded in tapping into elements that were emotionally powerful first time around and remain so today. It's partly to do with scale; it's no coincidence that all these cars are small enough to feel friendly and approachable. It's partly to do with rounded shapes which also make them feel feminine and non-aggressive (although the Mini manages to have a little macho-swagger mixed in).

Enough about cars. Almost. Compare any of the above three with almost any other modern small car and you'll see the qualitative difference between those that might be perfectly well-designed, quality 'products' and those which appear to have 'soul'.

If the soulful approach works for cafés and cars, and even for banks, I'd suggest that it has got to be worth pursuing for your business. But how do you do it?

I suggest a long walk.

Seriously. And this is precisely the exercise that I'd like you to carry out now.

Brand Builder Workout

You need to allow yourself at least two hours for this exercise, ideally three or four. So if you can't fit it in today or tomorrow, then don't try to rush it. Instead make a date with yourself to spend half a day sometime in the next week or fortnight.

Please don't try to do this exercise in a hurry. If you do, I can guarantee that it won't work. And please don't be tempted to skip this stage of our 30-day process. This is one of the most important stages of all.

I actually do want you to go for a walk. Alone. It can be country or city or a mixture of the two. Make it circular ideally, so that you are on a continual journey, rather than going somewhere then coming back.

If walking is impractical or impossible for you, you can try something else, like a long bus ride or a train journey. Driving yourself won't work so well. You need to be able to let your mind drift, which is a bit dangerous when you're driving.

This is a kind of meditation, I guess, but I like to think of it as action meditation because you're on the move. And bear with me here; this is an act of imagination, using the power of story to bring your brand to life in your imagination and your soul.

All you need to take with you is a little notebook or some pieces of paper, and a pen or pencil. No other equipment required. Please try to leave your mobile phone at home!

Before you set off I'd like you to sit down and write down these twelve questions in your notebook. Don't try to answer them at this point. We're going to avoid the temptation to jump to conclusions too early. But do write them out in full.

1. If my business (my brand) was not a business at all but a character from another period of history, what kind of character would it be?

2. What does this character look like, dress like, sound like? And what is their name?

3. Where does your character come from? Where do they live?

4. What does this character believe in? What are his or her values and passions?

5. What is your character's 'mission' or 'quest'? What are they determined to achieve?

6. What is it that frightens your character most about their mission. Why might they be reluctant to set out on this adventure?

7. Does your character have to go on a journey to achieve their mission? Where will they go and what places will they pass through on the way?

8. What kind of challenges will your character face along the way? What will be the biggest challenge of all?

9. What resources does your character have to draw on? What tools and supplies, whether 'real-world' or magical?

10. What friends, supporters or mentors can your character call upon for help? Who are they, and how can they be summoned?

11. What will your character bring back from their quest and what impact will it have on their friends, family and community?

12.   When people talk about your character and their great adventure, what will they say? How will they describe what happened?

Just a bit of clarification about your 'character'. I'm not talking about a famous character (real or fictional) but rather a type of person. I'm only going to give you a few examples here, because I don't want to influence your imagination, but what I mean is for you to picture a character as vividly as possible. Perhaps your character is a Victorian explorer, or a Japanese Geisha, or a cowboy, or a medieval troubadour? Or a Renaissance artist? Or a Suffragette? Or a Hobbit?

During the course of your walk I want you to imagine this character as vividly as possible. Make identifying this person the first task of your journey as you walk. If you can draw you might want to sketch him or her. You might find it easier to write a description. You may be able to conjure them up so powerfully that they come alive in your head, but it's still a good idea to scribble a few notes to look back at later.

What you're doing here is a version of an approach often called 'the hero's journey'. This journey is a metaphor, of course, a way of tapping into something very powerful in human nature: the power of myth, legend and story.

As you walk, and when you stop for a coffee or lunch along the way, keep thinking about your 'hero' and his or her journey. Look back over the 12 questions and scribble a few notes in response to each.

It's important that you give yourself enough time to do this alone and without pressure from other concerns. You are trying to free your imagination here. The whole idea might feel uncomfortable to you. If that's the case, don't worry. That's a normal, businesslike response. But don't let that concern overwhelm you.

Believe me when I say that your brand will be the stronger in the long run for the time and faith that you put into this exercise.

During the course of your walk, try to make some notes in answer to each of the 12 questions, and then when you return I suggest that you put your notes carefully aside for the rest of the day. Ideally avoid discussing the exercise with anyone for the moment. Just let it all sit there in your imagination overnight.

A day or two after your walk, get the notes out and take another look at them.

Now I want you to do part 2 of this exercise. I'd like you to think (and to write down) how the hero's journey that you have imagined can be brought to life in your business and your brand. It might help to think about these specific questions:

1. How might the adventure that you've imagined make your customers' experience more exciting, more enjoyable, more fulfilling. What will they experience that is unlike what your competitors provide?

2. If your brand is indeed a 'hero', what kind of things do you want your customers to say and think and feel about it?

3. How will your team members need to behave in order to live up to the 'legend' you've created?

4. How will you lead your team like a real hero? What will you do to inspire them and to allay their fears on the journey?

5. How will you remind yourself of the quest that you're on so you can remember what it's all about when times are tough or confusing?

This strange exercise is not about trying to create a brand that looks archaic or like a fairytale or a comic book. This is an exercise in imagination, a metaphor. But it is about unleashing a quality which brilliant brands understand and lesser ones don't: the quality of myth-making which is so intrinsically human.

Keep your notes tucked away safely and look at them from time to time. I think they will have more power than you might imagine.

Now, ready for your walk?

REAL BRAND STORY

BeWILDerwood

Tom Blofeld and Simon Egan, founders of BeWILDerwood, and their brand visionary, John Lyle of Purple Circle, explain how they used the power of imagination to create a world-class tourist attraction from scratch.

BeWILDerwood started as an idea by two friends. Tom Blofeld, a landowner, and Simon Egan, a former sculptor and trusted friend to Tom. Faced with the prospect of a declining farm income and some beautiful but unused woods, the two conceived a plan to build a treehouse adventure park.

At this point, the expert partners come in. In creating BeWILDerwood there were six key areas to manage:

First we needed the product. If we got that wrong, people might try us once, but they simply wouldn't come back. They'd tell their friends too, so the business would be doomed from the start. We selected a team that we knew would create safe, beautifully constructed woodland structures, with the potential to be appealing and engaging for children.

Next came the branding. John (Lyle) drew up a set of brand values that became the guiding principles behind many of our decisions. From some very simple sketches and a name supplied by the illustrator Stephen Pearce, the BeWILDerwood logo was born and began to grow.

John then extended this into the wording for the signage, the website and the literature. The decision was taken to create a single powerful image for the whole season. It was one born out of necessity as we needed materials but hadn't built the park yet, but it proved a very wise one, as the image of a child hanging upside down in a wild, wild wood and against a colourful treehouse backdrop, became the signature by which we were known.

Then came the books. Tom (Blofeld), walking around the park under construction one day, blurted out that when he was little, a strange group of creatures used to play alongside him (in his rather fertile imagination, of course) and then followed the remark by striding off purposefully to write a book about them. A few days later the initial results were shared around.

The product actually changed halfway through build, on the advice of Nick Farmer, the renowned theme park 'magician' and his illustrator Steve Pearce. They brought Tom's characters to life and added some 'pixie dust' to the original designs.

The next few months were a frantic exercise in trialing and refining. All of the team had their say and all input was valued. The project stayed incredibly true to its initial brand values, despite thousands of distractions.

Decisions were made because they felt right, not because they followed any conventional wisdom. The design evolved through all of our kids playing with the work in progress and telling us their brutally honest thoughts.

Our fourth element is promotion. Kate Moorfoot of Jungle PR built a campaign to attract local and national press to our two-day opening event, set for the weekend of May bank holiday. This date was set deliberately to coincide with the marsh coming to life and-he native irises in full bloom. A small detail but, on arrival, one that made the walk through BeWILDerwood simply beautiful.

Journalists brought their kids too, and between us we decided to let the kids be our judges. Instead of accompanying the journalists on a formal tour, they were left to run wild in the woods with their kids and literally 'live test' the park.

As the kids came out laughing and whooping, we asked them what they thought. "The best place in the world," said one. "Amazing, I want to live here," said the next. As the kids rolled out exhausted and happy, the parents went home to write page upon page of fabulous glowing copy and the world of BeWILDerwood was born.

But there are still two more points that we believe made BeWILDerwood the brand that it is. One came later, and one we only realized later.

The one we realized later was timing. BeWILDerwood opened in the May after the *Dangerous Book for Boys* was the huge Christmas number one bestseller. Concerns about the time our children spend in front of their games consoles and the threat to their health of childhood obesity combined with the parental fear about them playing outside all added to the mix.

BeWILDerwood answered all of these questions in one. Like many phenomena of their day, the timing was simply perfect. It feels like this is a generational change, too, and good old-fashioned imaginative play is back to stay. If our kids are to stay healthy, they have to learn to play outside again.

And the final factor was learning to trade properly. Too many great ideas are let down by really poor execution or careless management. Tom, Simon (Egan) and their team actively manage the staff, the children's and the parents' experience, day in and day out. They listen to what their customers say and then set about implementing improvements.

Day II

WHO DON'T YOU WANT TO SELL TO?

Often the most effective way to identify your market and your customers is to pinpoint those people to whom you don't want to appeal. In this chapter we're going to take a look at 'enemy' customers so we can (as the CID might say) eliminate them from our enquiries.

This might sound a little counter-intuitive and negative at first, but I promise you it works, and it's an important step in refining your brand. Why? Because **the simple truth is that your brand can never, simply cannot, just can't, appeal to all people**.

To achieve the impossible nirvana of being loved by everyone you would have to become so flexible, so malleable, so nebulous in fact, as to become meaningless to everyone too. Which is a logical absurdity. So let's not even try.

That's 'everyone' out of the way. But there are large and dangerous sub-sets of 'everyone' too, which we also need to cut down to size. You can't, for example, set out just to appeal to teenagers, or even to teenagers who drink coffee, or even teenagers who drink coffee but who hate Starbucks (although that's getting closer as a workable audience). The reason it's getting closer to useful is because it has introduced 'attitude' into the description, and attitude reflects emotion, and emotion lies at the heart of brand.

Anyway, what I've found is that it is frequently faster and more effective in the real world to work in reverse: to identify the people you don't want to appeal to.

I'll use my own business as an example, and I'll try to explain why I've made that choice in each case. I'm talking here about my consultancy/advisory work, where I advise companies, charities and so on about their brand strategy. Here are the people I've decided I don't want to sell to.

- Projects that I personally find ethically questionable (arms trade and tobacco are obvious ones but there are others).

- Projects where the client is not genuinely open to the potential need to change.

- Organizations that do not value my personal experience and views.

- Projects where the methodology has been decided in advance (unless there is some room for change).

- Projects where the key measure of the value of my intervention is in 'hours' as opposed to 'effectiveness'.

- Organizations that are only 'dabbling' in brand and don't genuinely believe in its importance.

- Projects that are built around the 'cheapest' process rather than the most effective solution.

Now that's not a very long list, but having the list gives me two distinct benefits.

First, it enables me to be clear, without the need to constantly re-assess which business opportunities I want to pursue and which I don't. That's not to say that I don't sometimes makes mistakes, ignore the list, and waste time and resources running after opportunities that I shouldn't. I recently tendered for a project from a local authority which was ostensibly about 'brand strategy'. It was a classic 'tender' and I knew in my heart that I shouldn't have gone for it because it failed my 'who don't I want to work for?' test on several counts. Needless to say I wasn't appointed, and it was clear afterwards (in fact it was clear before but I chose to ignore the evidence) that I was a bad match for the project. The client had decided on a very particular methodology and process (rather than deciding on a clear aim). The client wanted to know a detailed costing breakdown of hours and activity in advance (which I could not provide). And so on. It's not that the client had the 'wrong' approach *per se*. That's not my point. It's that this project wasn't right for me (nor I for it) and yet I still went after it, even though I knew really that it was not 'on-brand' for me.

Now my business is of a particular kind: consultancy. But the same principle applies whatever field you are in.

Let's imagine that we're setting up a small boutique hotel in a small city. Let's make a list of 'enemy' customers. This is just my list, of course. Yours will be different, I'm sure.

People that my hotel is *not* aimed at. . .

- People who are always looking for the cheapest deal.

- People for whom money is no object at all.

- People who have seen everything and are surprised and delighted by little.

- People who like their hotels modern, minimalist and bland.

- People who think trouser-presses in bedrooms are essential.

- People who expect 'adult' channels on their TV.

- People who tend to be loudly demanding of hotel staff and do not treat them with respect.

That might be a quirky list, but I hope that you can see how it helps to define my imagined boutique hotel brand. If the above are the people at whom my hotel is not aimed, I begin to form a picture of who it is really for. Writing this, right now, I'm sitting in a Costa coffee shop which is itself within a Waterstone's bookshop. I'm quite a fan of Waterstone's, although not an unqualified one (mainly because Waterstone's and other chains have prospered fundamentally through the rather sad demise of the small independent bookstore which is now an endangered species, if not actually close to extinction). Anyway, I'm only speculating here, and Waterstone's themselves might disagree with me, but I'll hazard a list of 'enemy' customers for this particular brand.

- People who only want to buy books when undertaking train or plane journeys.

- People who just haven't got time to browse and look at and handle books.

- People who think bookshops should be like old-fashioned libraries, hushed and formal.

- People who think there are just too many books published.

- People who think serious 'literature' is too important to be mixed up with entertainment fiction.

- People who have an elitist outlook about literature.

The people who fit any of the descriptions above could never feel comfortable in Waterstones.

Brand Builder Workout

Okay, now it's your turn. This exercise can be carried out alone, of course, but as with many exercises in this book I suggest that you'll get more value from it, as well as finding it more fun and more stimulating, if you work with someone close to you and your brand.

It's a simple set-up. Just write down in the centre of as big a piece of paper as you can find, the following:

OUR BRAND DOES NOT WANT TO APPEAL TO PEOPLE WHO...

Now, all around that big headline just start to describe your 'enemy' customers. You might only have two or three, but I suggest that if you can identify somewhere between five and 20 kinds of 'enemy' customers then you will be drilling deep enough into your brand meaning to be describing something very meaningful.

Throughout the exercise avoid the temptation to go into 'positive' mode. Stick with the people you don't want as customers for as long as possible.

A big caveat here: don't just use easy 'labels' for your 'brand enemies' but try to actually describe attitudes and outlooks.

If you wish you can then move to a part 2 of this exercise, which is to try to describe what kind of people haven't ended up on your 'enemy' list. In other words, to use the negative outputs of the exercise to start to build a positive picture of who your ideal customers should be. But personally, I am cautious about going too far down this road. I'm not at all sure that any brand can really describe an 'ideal' customer, or even a number of different 'ideal' customers. To my mind, this becomes self-limiting, which is why I prefer this counterintuitive 'brand enemy' approach. Still, you might feel differently and, depending on your particular brand and your particular mindset, you might choose to make a parallel list of 'people to whom we do want to appeal'. Just be cautious about making this a limiting/exclusive list.

Day 12

EXPLORING YOUR BRAND THROUGH THE SIX-LEGGED SPIDER

B rands, like people, are unique: or at least they should be if they want to succeed. This chapter builds on some of the work you've already done on the elements of your brand purpose, but uses a slightly different approach to help you construct the essential chemistry of your brand which makes you different from everybody else on the planet.

That's not to say that being different is everything, but it is certainly an important starting point. It's self-evidently true that being different gives you some advantages. Visibility for one. If you're the same as everyone else, you'll have a disappointing tendency to disappear into the background. But it's not enough to be different, of course; you also need to be compelling, authentic and relevant. Compelling so that customers will be drawn towards you and your brand story. Authentic so that they can trust your story and believe in you. Relevant so you can make a connection with their lives, their needs and desires.

You've already done lots of the hard work asked for in this chapter, earlier in the book, that is to say you have generated and collected some of the 'data' from the work you've already done. We're going to add some more, and then we're going to test that data.

Take a look at the diagram below. In workshops I habitually refer to it as the six-legged spider. This is absurd, of course, but people seem to remember it, and frequently refer to the six-leg spider diagram when talking to me about their brand. Absurdity sometimes helps a bit in remembering things (including brands).

This chapter is really just one big exercise, and it will help a lot if you do that exercise on the biggest sheet of paper you can find. Flip-chart paper is big enough (just) and I recommend it for this. There's something physically and therefore mentally different about working on a big field! Another of my favourite approaches with this exercise is to hang a great big paper tablecloth across a dining room table. As with many of the exercises in this book, you can do it alone, but it will be much more effective if you work with a few trusted people.

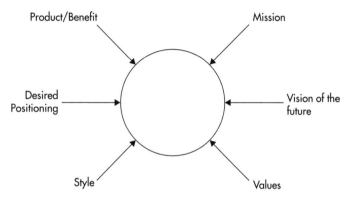

The six-legged brand spider.

Brand Builder Workout

Product/Benefit

Top left of the above diagram is a box marked PRODUCT/BENEFIT. This box is all about what your brand actually does (which I'm calling **product**, although it includes services and anything else you do too), and why it matters (in other words the **benefit** of whatever kind it brings to customers).

Underneath this header you need to capture in simple notes exactly that: what you do and why it matters. Now the degree of focus matters here. One of the things you do as a brand/business is likely to be filing. Or making the coffee. Now those things might be important, but if you include that sort of level of detail we're going to be building our brand in 30 years rather than 30 days. So please ignore all the stuff like filing and coffee (unless, of course, your brand happens to be a secretarial service or a coffee shop). In other words, we're trying to collect the descriptors which are pertinent to your particular business.

Watch out, though, for the opposite end of the telescope. Just as we don't have room for all the microscopic detail of business life, we also want to avoid (under this header anyway) the great big, world-changing, macro-macho statements about your brand. There's room for those later.

Desired Positioning

Positioning is a very popular concept in marketing and branding. It's interpreted in various ways. My preferred definition is that desired positioning is about how you want your brand to be perceived 'relative' to other brands inside the mental world of the customer. Positioning is all about the 'relative' rather than the 'absolute'.

There's a lot more about positioning in a subsequent chapter but, for now, just to give you a few examples these are typical positioning words: CHEAP, EXPENSIVE, PREMIUM, BESPOKE, LUXURY, INNOVATIVE, ADVANCED, RELIABLE, TRUSTED, GUARANTEED, LOCALLY SOURCED, DESIGNER, EFFICIENT, BEAUTIFUL, STYLISH, FAST, CARBON NEUTRAL, FAIR-TRADE, ETHICAL, PROFESSIONAL

Remember, when you do this exercise you are projecting into the future: this is all about what you want your customers and prospects to think and feel. It's your 'desired positioning'. Positioning can be about any aspect of your brand (product quality, service, price, technical aspects, design). Try to stick to single words or short phrases for this leg of the spider.

Style

If positioning is all about the space you occupy in people's heads and hearts, then 'style' is more concerned with how your brand will actually interact with and relate to your customers. Style is less about what your brand does than how it does it.

Completing this part of the exercise follows the same pattern though; you just need to capture words and short phrases that describe your brand's desired/intended style of interaction. Typical 'style' words include: FRIENDLY, APPROACHABLE, COOL, CLINICAL, TRENDY, FASHION-ABLE, TRADITIONAL, QUIRKY, ASPIRATIONAL, CHARMING, HELPFUL, RESERVED, ACADEMIC.

Only you can know what you want your style of interaction to be. And as with all these things there is absolutely no right or wrong.

Mission

Mission statements used to be terribly fashionable in the corporate world. Now, happily, they've fallen from grace. Like most people I think of big corporate mission statements as empty vessels. You still come across them from time to time, at the front-end of annual reports, or on dusty and faded posters and banners in open-plan offices. Sometimes you see corporate mission statements turned into to rather lame positioning lines (slogans).

So, mission statements are problematic. Nevertheless, the simple concept of a mission statement is at its core a helpful one, so let's not throw the proverbial baby out with its bath-water.

Somehow we need to express, or at least find some way of recording, our big, grand sense of our importance (and the importance of our brand). So I tell my workshop participants that this is the place where they can collect their big statements.

Mission is the space for the big thought, what I sometimes refer to as 'the meaning beyond the money'. Your mission might be described as the thing that sends you into the fray every day.

By way of example: if you sell bicycles your mission might include helping to save the planet from carbon emissions (or at least to play a role in that). If you're a coffee shop you might be on a mission to improve the lot of coffee producers in plantations on the other side of the world. Your mission might be closer to home. Maybe you want your neighbourhood to have an independent local source of financial advice. Or vegetables. Maybe you just want middle aged men to dress better. Maybe you want the world to be more colourful. Or quieter. Or...

I'll leave it to you and your team to be as dramatic, impassioned and world-changing as you like here. This is the place for it. Don't be shy, because some of this mission stuff will be very useful at the next stage.

Vision of the Future

Don't mix up mission with vision. Words are funny things, are they not? The more 'conceptual' they are, the more one has to define them carefully before using them. For this exercise, 'vision' simply means how you see things developing in the future. It's helpful to put a timescale on 'future'. It's up to you entirely, but I would suggest something like six months, one year, two years and five years. There's no right way to set that timescale, but just bear in mind that we are going to try to paint a mental picture of what your brand will look like in the future.

But what do we mean by 'look like'? I mean a snapshot of a possible positive future. As with the positioning part of this exercise we're talking 'desired' future here. This isn't the place for pessimism.

Try to describe your future under some someheadings like these:

- Geography (where will you be located, what territory or territories will you cover?)

- Employees (how many people will be working in your brand and what will they be doing?)

- Reputation (how well known will you be and what will people be saying about you?)

- Competition (who will you be competing with, who will be your brand peers?)

It's important to remember when you do this not to fall into the trap of exaggeration. Optimism is appropriate, but don't feel pressured to imagine a future in which you are a world-dominant market-leader if the brand you are creating is simply not of that nature or scale. There is no requirement to be a global brand, or even a national brand, in order to be a great brand. Some of the world's most special and most successful brands trade in their own neighbourhoods and are virtually unknown outside that neighbourhood. If they are successful on their own terms and bring satisfaction to their customers and a sustainable living and fulfillment to their owners and employees then they are successful brands. Big isn't always beautiful.

But it's good to look into the future positively, for one very important reason among many others. If you imagine the future of your brand positively and paint a mental picture such as I suggest, and then you find that picture unappealing in some way, then you need to take a reality check right away. If you've described a successful brand to yourself and it somehow doesn't excite you or satisfy you emotionally, then perhaps there's something about your brand ambitions which is out of tune with you as a person.

If this book protects someone from working hard for years and years in pursuit of a dream which won't make them happy, then it will have been worthwhile. Be honest with yourself about your plans and your future.

Values

Well, this bit should be easy. I promised that you'd already done some of the hard work. Maybe you thought I meant more. I know you've had to work pretty hard in this chapter. Sorry. We've already covered values though. So all you need to do is dump that data from the previous values exercise under the 'values' heading here. There, that was easy.

///

In the next chapter you're going to use all the words and phrases that you've attached to the legs of your spider, to distil the real, essential DNA of your brand.

Day 13

REFINING YOUR UNIQUE BRAND ESSENCE

At the centre of the six-legged spider diagram you created in the last chapter lies the body of the spider: the magic circle! Inside this little circle (although I recommend you expand it to the size of a whole flip-chart sheet to work with comfortably) we are going to put the juice-with-no-pips, the essence, the best stuff, the magic elements from everything you've collected under your six headings.

This isn't a difficult exercise to do in practical terms, but a word of warning: it's one of the toughest things you'll do intellectually and emotionally in creating your brand. It requires you to be really cool, really objective, and really, really honest with yourself.

A successful conclusion to this exercise won't be a circle crammed to bursting with dozens of words and phrases. On the contrary, a successful conclusion will be when you can look at what's in the circle and say: "yep, that's it, that's the good stuff!"

With that thought in mind, then let's proceed. As promised, it's an easy one to do practically.

Brand Builder Workout

Simply look at each one of the words and phrases under each of the headings on your six-legged spider chart, and put each one through a simple test by asking the following four questions. Remember: to get into the magic circle, each word or phrase has to pass all four questions (well the first three anyway... we can cut ourselves a bit of slack on question 4, as you'll see when you get to it):

1. ***Is it true, or at the very least, achievable?***   Is the word or phrase you're looking at here really true or is it just wishful thinking? We'll allow things to pass this test if they are 'achievable' (i.e. you are confident that you are going to make them true, soon). Tim Smit, founder of The Eden Project, has a nice phrase for this: 'future truths'. Things which might not be tangible reality right now, but they are surely going to be!

As with this whole exercise, though, you've got be honest and objective. If you're working with others, as I recommend, make sure everyone in the group agrees that your word or phrase passes the 'true or achievable' test. We don't want to let any emperors wearing new clothes into our magic circle.

2. ***Is it interesting (to the customer)?*** An idea can be perfectly true and yet screamingly dull, can it not? Or a concept can be fascinating to you as the brand owner but utterly unimportant and uninteresting to a potential customer. Ask yourself, if you were a customer, would you care? Would you be even momentarily engaged by this truth? If not, don't put it in the magic circle. Remember, we're looking for the good stuff.

3. ***Is it commercially relevant?*** Does the word or phrase you're considering have a relevance to a commercial transaction between you and your customer, or is it just a 'nice to know'. Is it likely to make a difference to their decision to buy from you as opposed to from someone else? Be honest, be tough. We only want to put the most powerful stuff in the magic circle.

4. ***Is it differentiating (i.e. not the same same as the competition)?*** This is both the most important and challenging question and, ironically perhaps, the one on which you can allow yourself a bit of leeway. It's desperately important because being different from the competition (as we've said numerous times in this book) is rule one in branding. Being different, distinctive, individual, outstanding in some way, is a hugely important element for you and for every brand. But it's also true that difference can come from the way you tell your brand story: it isn't solely dependent on material difference. So, by way of example, imagine you're a painter and decorator. You might, actually/factually/materially be pretty much identical in what you do, how you do it and what you charge for it, as another painter and decorator not very far away from you. That doesn't mean you can't have a differentiated brand, because you might just find a way to tell a more engaging, compelling and distinctive 'story' than the other guy. Differentiation can come in many guises, so look at your words and phrases from different angles when you get to this question. I tend to give concepts the benefit of the doubt on this question and to let things pass into the circle, *providing* I have some sense that a differentiated story might be a possibility.

To sum up, we only put words and phrases into the magic circle if they are: **true** (or at least qualify as 'future truths'); **interesting**; **relevant**; and if they are either **differentiating** in and of themselves or if they have the potential to be so through the telling of the brand story.

If you've done this exercise honestly and rigorously you'll have a circle with words and phrases which really do begin to define your brand and what makes it unique. If in the unlikely event that you have just one or two words in the circle, then you should not be downhearted. Those few words will give your brand its distinctive power.

Stick this piece of paper somewhere prominent in your workspace; let it be your talisman as we move forward.

Day 14

UNDERSTANDING BRAND 'POSITIONING'

Positioning, as the word implies, is about where you want your business to be: but it doesn't mean in the geographical sense. You know the saying 'location, location, location' of course, which is applied to houses as well as to businesses. In the latter case, the thought is that where you choose to locate your shop, café, hotel or whatever is the most important element in determining its success. Whether that's true or not is another matter, but 'positioning' in a brand sense doesn't refer to where on the ground you put your business, but instead to where in people's heads you want to place it.

You know the popular saying that something is 'simply the best'? Of course you do. On numerous occasions over the years I have come across people who want to describe their business, product or brand as 'simply the best'. There is obvious pride and loyalty in this approach. But as a branding approach it simply won't do, and the reason that it won't do is in part down to the concept of positioning.

Positioning is a 'relative' concept. In other words it's about the space your brand occupies in the hearts and minds of your audience relative to other comparable brands. No brand exists in a vacuum. There are always others around somewhere. That's a key problem with 'simply the best'. It's an absolute term rather than a relative one and is, in effect, completely meaningless.

So before we go on to examine how you can really use positioning to your advantage, please make a solemn promise to yourself never to describe your brand as 'simply the best' or in any other terms that make such an absolute and therefore insubstantial claim. No matter how good you think you are. No matter, when it comes down to it, how good you actually are. The brutal truth is that **you cannot be a brand in any sort of useful sense if you claim to be 'simply the best'.**

Okay, that's out of the way, so what is positioning exactly and how do you do it? Well, at the risk of sounding rather Zen-like, **your brand position is not really something you do. It's more something you are**. But that's not to say you can't choose what you are. Of course you can, and you must, or someone else will. In fact, your brand position is absolutely not in the hands of fate. It's entirely in your hands, unless and until you don't manage it, which is when other people (not all of them on your side) will manage it for you.

Let's imagine that you are opening a bicycle shop. You're not going to sell anything at all except bicycles and their accessories, and you're going to sell a pretty wide range of 'types' of bicycle. You'll sell modern ones and traditional/retro ones. You'll sell tourers and city bikes, mountain bikes and out and out racers. But you've decided that you'll only sell the really good makes of bike in each type.

Imagine now that just around the corner from you is a sports equipment shop. A good one, which actually sells equipment, not just sports-style clothes. So, for example, it sells cricket bats and helmets, skis and accessories, gym equipment from small weights to home gyms. It also sells (annoyingly, you're inclined to think) a small range of bicycles. Even more annoyingly, it seems to be imitating some of the more specialist kinds of bikes that you sell.

You've discovered that there is a small but growing market for 1950s-style American bikes with their strange curving frames and high-rise handlebars. You're stocking the real stuff, from the States, and within a few weeks the sports shop round the corner is stocking that style of bike too, and cheaper! But theirs aren't the iconic American brand but an unknown brand of bike in roughly the same style. You're also very proud to be your town's only stockist of a classic and prestigious British bike brand that makes 'ladies' and 'gents' bicycles which have a timeless English style about them. They've even got wicker baskets on the front! But, darn it, the sports shop round the corner is soon selling bikes that are superficially similar. Although they're not the prestige brand that you stock.

Should you be downhearted by these developments? No. On the contrary, this is actually good for your brand. And why? Because of positioning.

Remember that I explained that positioning is a relative concept. Well, there are two important aspects of that relativity on display here. They're both important and they're both (surprisingly perhaps) good for your brand.

First, your bike shop has a very clear positioning compared to the sports equipment shop. You are a specialist, they are generalists. You have prestige and iconic brands. They stock 'imitations'. You are expensive because you sell 'premium' brands. They are relatively cheap. You and your people are doubtless passionate, focused and hugely knowledgeable about bicycles. They know quite a bit about lots of different sports.

Second, the fact that they are there, virtually on your doorstep, throws your relative positioning into brilliant relief, which is a real brand win for you. Because you should now be able to demonstrate very clearly the differences between your specialist service and the advice and aftercare that (hopefully) goes with it. And your customers can see for themselves the detailed differences between your prestige brands and your competitor's budget imitations. Of course, if your potential customers can't afford your products and buys from your competitor purely on grounds of substantial price difference, then they were arguably not really your potential customers at all.

Your position is clear, and because it's clear you can explain it, promote it and defend it against attack from competitors and from customers who want you to be something different.

Of course, when you are choosing your position you must look at more than one competitor. Perhaps there's another specialist bike shop on a little street corner outside the centre of town. That guy really knows his cycling onions and he sells consistently to people who could be described as real bike enthusiasts. Don't be frightened of this competitor either. Your position is quite different and clear. His shop is part workshop and part parts-store with barely enough room to swing a cat in let alone demonstrate the attributes of several different bikes. Your shop is big enough for families to browse in. His shop demands a special trip to the suburbs. Yours can be visited when a family is in town on a weekend afternoon.

That's not to say the other little shop can't thrive too. It does, and long may it continue. The point is that it occupies a different brand position from you. And it's being in a different position that's important. **The danger in positioning is in attempting to occupy the same position as someone else**, especially if that someone else is better established, better resourced and better branded than you. You might survive as a business, but life will always be a struggle.

You can see that positioning is multifaceted; it's not just a simple matter of being cheaper or more expensive than your competitors, nor just about a wider range, or more specialist knowledge. It might not be about any of these particular factors. That will depend on what kind of business you are in. Only you can know that and only you can decide what factors are important.

But that isn't as difficult as it may sound, as I hope the following exercise will demonstrate.

Brand Builder Workout

Take a look at the set of little grids below, which shows this exercise in action using the example of the three bicycle shops. On the left-hand side of each grid you'll see a horizontal rectangular box. And in each one is a key attribute of the 'positioning' of our imaginary bicycle shop.

The first is 'brands sold', then 'focus', 'specialist knowledge', 'price range' and so on. And as you can see, each little grid consists of a series of boxes, each with its own heading.

ATTRIBUTE

BRANDS SOLD	Luxury	Specialist	Popular	Budget
FOCUS	Specialist cycles	Range of bikes, just bikes	Sports gear inc' bikes	Bikes and auto parts
SPECIALIST KNOWLEDGE	High	Moderate	Poor	
PRICE RANGE	Luxury	Premium	Competitive	Cheap
AFTER CARE	Comprehensive	Normal	None	
SHOP ENVIRONMENT	Bright spacious	Small cosy	Crowded	Cramped
CONVENIENCE	Another town	Town centre	Suburb	

Your bike shop brand positioned in available territory.

In the case of brands sold you'll see the boxes are labelled: luxury, specialist, popular, and finally budget.

BRANDS SOLD	♥ Luxury	Specialist **CS**	♥ Popular	Budget **SE**

A map on which to position your bike shop.

If you go back to imagining you run the bicycle shop we looked at earlier, you can now draw a little heart (or any other symbol you like) in one or more of these boxes. The shop I described seems to me to deserve a heart symbol in two boxes in this case: luxury and popular.

But plotting your shop on this grid is only the first half of the task. Where would you put your two competitors, let's call them SE (for sports equipment) and CS (for corner shop). Personally, I'd put SE in budget, as I've shown, and CS in specialist. So far so good, you are clearly the only one of the three occupying the luxury and popular boxes. Good positioning.

Take a look at the rest of the grids for the bike shop scenario and I hope you'll see that our imagined store is pretty well positioned, occupying a quite distinctive place which it can call its own.

I could have added other attributes, but these will do for now. And note that some attributes use fewer boxes than others. There's no rule about this. You only need as many boxes as it takes to describe the possible variants.

Now it's your turn, with your brand.

Here's a set of empty grids for you to use with your brand and your competitors. The toughest part of the exercise is choosing the attribute titles, and to help you do this, just focus on what you think are the important factors in your kind of business. Is price a factor? What about location? Or geographical reach? Or target audience? You should be able to put headers by at least four of the grids below.

ATTRIBUTE

An empty map for you to position your own brand.

Now you need to apply a measure to each; in other words, to give a title to each of the boxes in each grid. If one of your grids is labelled price, then your boxes might be labelled: luxury, premium, competitive, cheap.

You can use whatever words you like, of course. The important thing is that their meaning is clear to you. You can then do the final part of the exercise, which is to plot first your brand and then one, two or more of your competitors on the grids.

Doing this whole exercise across, say, four or five attributes with two or three competitors will take you a little while. But please persist. Not only will you enjoy (I hope) the stimulus of thinking in such depth about the desired position of your brand, but you'll also end up a great deal wiser about whether or not your desired position is likely to be successful for you.

///

It's one thing to know your position relative to other brands, but it's another thing to use that knowledge. There are two broad and potentially exciting ways that you can utilize this secret knowledge! I call it 'secret knowledge', by the way, because it's a fact, sadly, that the vast majority of people running small businesses and organizations have not got the first idea of their brand position. Not because it's that difficult to work out, but because they've never asked the question. In my view, trying to run a brand of any kind without first thinking about (and subsequently constantly monitoring) your brand position can be likened to trying to pass the ball in a football match whilst wearing a blindfold and therefore without having any real sense of where you are on the pitch, let alone where your team-mates and your opponents are. For a superbly talented, instinctive player this might not be an absolutely impossible task but you've got to admit it would severely hamper their chances of making the pass.

The first way to use your secret knowledge is covertly. In other words, you know where you are and where your competitors are and you can use that knowledge to monitor, nurture and fine tune your brand as you go along. To go back to our bike shop: there's nothing to stop you (if the demand is there) from introducing an entry-level range of bikes. You might be able to identify and source brands that are stylish and premium in their own right but which carry a slightly lower price tag, enabling you to stay positioned clearly differently from your sports shop competitor, but nevertheless allowing you to pick off some of their (price sensitive) customers.

The second way to utilize positioning is overtly: in other words to tell the world about it loudly and proudly. Perhaps the most famous example of all of overt positioning in modern branding is actually pretty vintage now, but a good example nonetheless.

In the USA the car hire firm Hertz was always the market leader, practically from when the car hire industry began. Hertz were naturally proud of their market leader position and it gave them a real edge: success after all has a wonderful way of breeding success. Second in the market was Avis. You probably know the rest of the story: Avis campaigned for years with the idea that as second in the market place it always tried that bit harder. Brilliant overt positioning. Brilliant because it made Avis's place in the market clear (leaving all other firms in the pack of also-rans) and brilliant because it provided Avis with a a clear position in customers' minds and hearts as a firm which was self-deprecating and devoted to customer service.

Bringing the thought bang up to date, as I write this chapter a storm is brewing in the advertising and marketing world in the UK because of a series of advertisements in London by the high street electronics chain Dixons. In its campaign, Dixons focuses on its position of offering a wide range of branded goods at value prices by taking a direct and very irreverent swipe at luxury stores such as Harrods and Selfridges. Without actually naming the upmarket stores, it identifies them cleverly and suggests that discerning customers should visit the 'posh' shops to try out the goods and then go to Dixons to purchase. All based around the strapline: Dixons, the last place you should go.

Once again, brilliant positioning that makes a virtue of being different from the competition and at the same time brings a bit of character to a brand that is generally seen as somewhat bland and characterless.

A word of caution, though, before we leave the subject of positioning. Although the Dixons ads achieve the positioning message with an irreverently witty approach (though that's not what Harrods thinks, since at the time of writing the Knightsbridge store is threatening to take legal action), attacking the competition is not generally a wise fact. As a rule of thumb, in fac,t I'd stay well away from mentioning the competition.

You'll see some supermarkets taking on their competition directly but their case is very particular. The ones taking this route are generally competing on price, not on positioning. In other words, these particular supermarkets (Asda, Tesco, Morrisons for example) are accepting that they pretty much have identical brand positionings which is why all they have left to brag about is price. You'll notice that Waitrose stays out of this price scrapping, focusing on quality and provenance instead.

If you want to use your positioning overtly, much better to do so with the self-confidence of Stella Artois (Reassuringly Expensive), or with the self-deprecating charm of the Victoria & Albert Museum (which knows full well it is one of the world's greatest museums) describing itself as a fantastic café with quite a nice museum attached.

REAL BRAND STORY

Bray's Cottage Pork Pies

Sarah Pettegree, Director of Bray's Cottage Pork Pies, talks about 'hand-making' a food brand with a distinctive positioning, almost literally on the kitchen table.

Bray's Cottage Pork Pies is a small Norfolk business hand-making high quality pork pies. We started in early 2007 and the pies have been featured in *The Times, The Independent, The Telegraph, Country Living*, a good handful of food magazines and have won *Great Taste Award* Gold Stars two years running. We have two main distribution channels: wholesale to delis, farm shops, pubs, restaurants, etc., and also direct to the public at Farmers Markets and events, plus a little mail order.

Life as a small food producer is all about hard work and keeping plates spinning, so the work I do on the brand and marketing is a fun part of the job, and I love and flourish on the creativity of it.

Apart from two sows and the smallholding, which belongs to Nell, my business partner, the pies started out with zero external investment (and have carried on that way), so to avoid spending money we didn't have all our branding and marketing has been created in-house. I built the website, designed the logo (a graphic designer friend eventually tidied it up in return for pies!), and wrote the copy.

I started with what we knew was an unusually good product and a set of values. The main product is a premium pork pie with onion marmalade. Pork pies are usually a cheap, downmarket product. Ours were made from our rare breed, outdoor pigs and tasted very different from commercial pies. We were keen that they appealed to women as well as men. When we were finding our 'voice' I spent time looking at a booklet produced by Innocent Smoothies (before they sold a stake to Coca Cola). I liked their sense of fun and honesty. And the design of the booklet looked spare, fresh and contemporary. It felt like the way we were.

The values were centered around treating the pigs with respect and making pork pies a food that was identified with quality and a sense of occasion rather than something eaten guiltily on a garage forecourt.

We had a bit of early indecision over the name, which has left us with an odd dual identity. The company was incorporated as Perfect Pie Ltd which resulted from a fabulous review of the pies that Giles Coren wrote in *The Times* when Nell still owned half of a farm shop that he wandered into. He called them 'the perfect pie'. I also built the website with perfectpie.co.uk as the URL. The other option was to name the pies after Nell's smallholding, Bray's Cottage. I was always drawn to that because of its links with the countryside and the farm, which was part of our story. On the other hand, we felt that a website name had to be easy to remember. So, having used Perfect Pie for the URL and the company name, and having been featured in *The Times* again we talked it over with our friend Pauline Kent who works in PR. She favoured Bray's Cottage as well so we switched the name of the pies to Bray's Cottage Pork Pies. Possibly not the ideal thing to have two identities, but we've coped.

We inadvertently struck lucky with our logo. I am an artist (not that I've done very much since the pies took over) and a few years before I'd done some prints based on a sow living at our local rural life museum. So we already had a simple line drawing to hand.

The fact that the logo featured a pig was deliberate. I wanted the pies to tell the story of their origins and make people think about where their food came from.

I've done hardly any deliberate PR work but it seems to be that once you have one national article under your belt then you are on journalists' radars and get approached. I understand their need for a story and try to make their lives as easy as possible by providing ideas, photos and information.

Frequently journalists find us via our website, www.perfectpie. co.uk. It's far from flashy but I wanted to make it simple, interesting and attractive. If it was slick and corporate it wouldn't reflect our identity as accurately. Without any particular understanding of SEO, we have always managed to be on page 1 or 2 of Google for 'pork pie' searches (out of about six million) and right at the top of the list for 'best pork pie'.

I also use Twitter with @Bray's_Cottage and have made contacts, been found by journalists and PRs, keep in contact with customers, had valuable help and advice and sold pies via Twitter. And it's something I can do easily whilst doing other work. In fact it's a bit of light relief. I keep the tone light, chatty and not pushy.

We are a very female company and value that as an asset and a way of differentiating the product from the general pie factory world. I'm keen on collaboration with other food producers and committed to supporting the food community. We are strongly associated with rural North Norfolk, making the pies in a converted flint stable a couple of miles from the sea. And the bottom line is that it has to be honest and has to be fun.

Day 15

CREATING THE NARRATIVE

Ibelieve that story (or narrative) is the most important single element in branding. It is story that will ultimately set you apart from all your competitors: the competitors who look a bit like you and sell similar 'stuff' (products, services, whatever) at roughly similar prices. The competitors who are really inferior but try to outgun you on price or speed. And even the competitors who are actually better than you right now, with better products, and even with better service. In successful branding, the power of story is the supreme magical force, the great differentiator.

This is true for two reasons. First, because branding really is, at its core, the craft and art of storytelling. Second, because in the modern world brands have come to play a story-telling role in our lives that has parallels with the myths, legends, folklore and even religious narratives of the past.

This chapter is about how you reveal, shape and communicate your brand story to set yourself apart from competitors and create a niche in your potential customers' hearts and minds.

First we need a few definitions. My trusty Chambers says. . . Actually, before we get to that, here's a story. In the front of my battered, bright red Chambers Twentieth Century Dictionary, there's a little hand-written dedication, clearly written with a fountain pen. It says 'To Simon, Happy Birthday, with all of my love, Sheila. 1978.'

Sheila gave me that dictionary on 10 September 1978 to be precise. It was my 20th birthday. Though it doesn't mention it in the dedication, we had been married less than eight weeks. We are still married. My daughter, in her twenties, says we must have been 'saddos'. Why else would a young wife give a young husband a dictionary as a 20th birthday present in the early weeks of their marriage? Not very sexy or romantic is it? But it is to me. And actually I don't want a new dictionary. Ever. Because this one isn't just full of words. This one's full of stories.

Reminds me of another one. A very good friend of ours from that era bought himself the same Chambers dictionary shortly afterwards. The apparent obsession with dictionaries stemmed from our shared ambitions as writers. However, my friend — who was always a bit cleverer than me — evidently did not feel the need to consult his dictionary as frequently as I did because he only discovered a couple of years later that his copy was incorrectly bound and was missing every page from the middle of the Ls to the middle of the Ps.

As stories go, neither of these is an award winner. But both are significant. The first allows me to brag that I've been married to my teenage sweetheart for more than 30 years. The second hints at my belief that sheer bloody hard work (in this case consulting the dictionary regularly) can deliver just as great a long term payoff as raw ability.

I've digressed to tell you these stories because I want you to start to digress; to put aside for a little while the pressures and concerns of running your business or your team or your organization, and to think a little about story. And remember, story is always personal.

Back to the definitions. Under the entry for 'story' Chambers says, more or less: *history; legend; a narrative of incidents in their sequence; a fictitious narrative; a tale; an anecdote; the plot of a novel or drama; a theme; an account; report; statement; allegation; a news article; a lie; a fib; to tell or describe historically; to relate; to adorn with scenes from history.*

Think about that list of definitions for a moment. Is this not a list of some of the most powerfully 'human' things that we humans engage in? Whether we are rich or poor, pessimists or optimists, entrepreneurs or labourers, story and the telling of stories is arguably what defines us. Over the millennia it has been story that we have used to make sense of our confusing world. Stories of how the world began. Stories of the gods creating and destroying, warring with each other, influencing our lives and our deaths. Stories of our great heroes, our great villains, our monsters, our romantic and tragic figures.

Now think about the modern, choice-filled, ever-changing world in which we live. In the wealthy developed world at least we face rather more benign challenges than our ancient (and even not so ancient) ancestors. Instead of the misery of living hand to mouth we now face what marketers call 'the misery of choice'. Which product, which service, which store, which online provider, which tariff? And how do we deal with that misery of choice?

Well, vast numbers of us do it by side-stepping the difficulty completely. The ancient Greek philosophers known as the Stoics said that all choice is misery, and the only way to avoid the misery of the human condition is to avoid making choices. Well, that's all very well for the Stoics, but I'm working on the assumption that you, and more importantly your customers, are in the habit of making choices all the time. But what is the clever side-step that so many of us use habitually, in the main without even thinking about it? You guessed it, it's 'brand'. **Brand simplifies choice so dramatically, so satisfyingly, so easily, that it's no wonder we use it so much**.

A few personal examples right off the top of my head:

- There may be many ways in which I can listen to a vast library of music free of charge whilst I work. There are probably a dozen or more facilities that offer me this in one way or another. There may be a hundred. I don't know. And I don't care. Because I've found Spotify.

- Looking back to when my children were small (they're all grown up now), there may have been several shoe manufacturers who made shoes that were carefully designed, manufactured and equally carefully fitted by experts to provide my children with the very best chance of growing up with healthy feet. There may have been. But I didn't have to go looking or choosing because I had found Start-rite.

- There are any number of solutions to the practical challenge: what kind of diary should I buy? Most diary purchases I would guess are pretty low on emotional involvement. It gets towards the last quarter of the year. You start to be told about weddings or other family events coming up in the following year. It's time to get a diary. Roughly around the same time the shops start stocking next year's diaries. You look at a few casually, choose the format that looks practical and select a colour or cover design that appeals. It's no big deal but you can still waste time choosing if you're a bit of a stationery geek like me. But I don't do this any more, because only one diary will do: Moleskine. They're more expensive than other diaries. They're mostly black. They're the only one.

- I'm planning to buy a compact motor home. Not a blooming great big one, but a relatively little one that Sheila and I can jump in to disappear for a long weekend or an unplanned week somewhere in the UK. There aren't that many manufacturers of compact motor homes, so the misery of choice in this case isn't caused by having to select from a vast array of competitors. No, in this case the misery is caused by the fact that the definitive small motor home was created more than 40 years ago and has never been bettered (in brand and story terms). The VW Campervan is so iconic, so aesthetically pleasing, so charming and so 'right' that I can't really bring myself to consider anything else. And yet those of my friends who know about such things say that these VWs are over-priced, under-powered, unreliable and very demanding of constant maintenance (they're old after all) and a pretty impractical and uncomfortable motoring option. They're probably right. Hence the misery. I don't really want anything else.

- There may be all kinds of practical reasons why I should choose a PC of some kind when I buy my next laptop. There may be technical advantages. There are certainly tempting financial advantages (almost any PC is cheaper than what I know I will buy). But I'm not interested and therefore I don't have to compare endless spec sheets and reviews. And why am I not interested? Because (if I haven't said so somewhere already) the answer is, of course, because I'm a Mac user. Think about how my misery of choice is dealt with in this case. Hundreds of manufacturers stripped out of the contest in an instant. I simply do not care what anyone else has to offer (no matter how advantageous it might actually be). From hundreds of manufacturers to just one. For me it is literally a one-horse race. All I have to do is choose the Mac I want at the time.

All of the above are about brand as the mechanism of choice, a mechanism which is so powerful that it achieves a brilliant quadruple-whammy!

1. It allows the particular product or service to stand out so far from all other competitors that they almost cease to exist in any effective sense.

2. It allows the particular product or service to charge a premium which actually makes it more, rather than less, appealing to the customer.

3. It allows the company concerned to continue to develop in its own individual way, pursuing even greater individuality and distinctiveness (putting ever greater stretches of clear blue water between itself and its competitors).

4. It doesn't just provide the customer with a satisfying purchase and experience. It doesn't just provide the rather prosaic quality

of 'peace-of-mind'. It goes beyond this to provide a deep-rooted sense of having found a 'story' which satisfies a human yearning for things to make sense. For hope as well as reassurance. For a sense of belonging, pride, enjoyment in participation. And so on. Please don't make the mistake of thinking that this is all getting a little too 'poetic'. This is how brands work. This is what will make your brand a success.

So, we need to get back to 'story'. Where does it fit, and how can you use it? Look again at my examples above. What do they have in common? It isn't massive advertising spend. True, Apple spends heavily on advertising but I've been a Mac user since the early 1990s and that's got very little to do with advertising. It isn't that they're hip and happening and aimed at just the youth market, or the high tech market, or the early adopter market, or any other market segmentation. It isn't that they're 'advanced' technologically. Apple is. Spotify is. But not the others. That's not the link. It isn't even product performance or other claims made about the product or the service. They all do make claims, but that isn't the point or the link between them.

The link is: story. Each one of these brands has found its way into my head/heart through story. Here's how:

Spotify A friend nagged me about Spotify for weeks. Telling me about the vastness of the library and the strange pleasure of being able to listen to half-forgotten or never-heard-before music without having to put your hand in your pocket. Spotify, he said, was a kind of musical adventure. I resisted. Until another music-fan friend said the same thing. I tried it out. I'm hooked. I now tell others, all the time. The story goes on being spread.

Start-rite It's a simple story about focus. Start-rite only, exclusively, makes shoes for children. From the first shoes a child wears, before it is even walking, to the first proper shoes, right through to first school shoes and so on. All the time with an obsessive dedication to making these shoes fit your child perfectly. There's a choice for you. Shoes that will enable your child's feet to grow healthily? Or some other kind.

Moleskine   Open a Moleskine diary or notebook and you'll find a little pocket built into the back cover. Handy for all kinds of things, from business cards to stamps to shopping lists. But when you buy it you'll find the pocket already has something in it: a little printed leaflet telling you the Moleskine story. Yes, they were originally made from moleskin, but that's not the real heart of the story: the best bit is that they were the chosen notebooks of Vincent Van Gogh and Ernest Hemingway. Van Gogh and Hemingway? Stories don't come much better than that. Why would I want any other notebook or diary?

VW campervans   Woodstock. Surfing. Hippies. Freedom. Cuteness. German technicians create a workhorse in the 1950s which was adopted by the love-children of the 1960s. And decades later they are still the fetish objects of the trapped suburban middle-aged baby-boomers. Freedom on four wheels with a pop-up roof. That's a story.

Apple   Arguably the greatest modern storytellers of all. Way back when the Mac was touted as 'the computer for the rest of us'. In other words, the computer for the non-geek, the computer that would set you free from technical gobbledegook. The computer equivalent of the Volkswagen. Great opening story, but one which became harder to believe as Apple struggled with loss of identity in its middle period. When I bought my first Mac in 1993 I was told Apple would soon be out of business. They had lost the plot and were doomed. But, lo and behold, they turn disaster into triumph. Founder Steve Jobs returns and, with a British designer, creates the paradigm-shifting iMac (remember the first ones in bright colours, looking like the 1950s meeting the 22nd century in a big bang of delicious and shocking design?). And 20 years later they are still the zenith of design brilliance. No other computer manufacturer comes even close in aesthetic and mystery. And in the sheer devotion of their customers. I described myself earlier as a Mac user. That's what we call ourselves. But user is an inadequate word. A better one would be devotee.

Five incredibly powerful stories. Now its your turn. I want you to do two exercises.

Brand Builder Workout

Pick four of your favourite brands and write their story as though you were telling it to a friend or relative about why you admire it so much. Don't dwell on product specs and other practical advantages. Your friend or relative will soon be bored if you do. Instead tell the 'story' as briefly as possible.

1. _____

2. _____

3. _____

4. _____

Now it's time for your story. Try writing your brand story. Say something about your origins if you like. Say something about you or another figurehead if that's relevant to you (it is for Apple and for Virgin, but not for VW or Start-rite). Say something about the passion that you feel and the tribulations that you have met and dealt with. Tell a story that makes you feel like a legend. Don't make it up. We're talking 'authenticity' here. But you are telling a story after all... feel free to exaggerate and dramatize and romanticize. Try to write something that makes you feel proud and excited. You're not making advertising here, so don't worry about your writing style or anything like that. What you are doing is bringing the power of story alive in your mind. Once you've articulated it to yourself like this you can then confidently articulate it to others. And then don't forget to tell this story to your customers and your potential customers. Remember, people love stories. Stories make your brand real.

Send me your story. I'd love to read it.

THE EXPERT VIEW

Tracy Kenny, Aviva

Last year I visited a pediatrician's office in the US. I know nothing of the doctors there; I was just looking after my sister's children while she took her 9-year-old in for a routine check-up. We played hairdressers on the floor on the right side of the reception desk, and then we left. Were the doctors competent? Did they listen? Did my niece have to wait for an appointment? I have no idea how they measure up to any of the traditional measures of a health care service. I didn't see a patient charter. And I certainly didn't see any abstract articulation of their values. But what I do know is this: that they had another waiting room on the left side of reception, for the sick kids. They separated out those who were well from those who were contagious. Without a word, a signal, or a glance from the staff, the surgery's story came through: we want kids to stay well.

Now even though nothing really happened, I used the word 'story' there. And it does count as a story, and not just because I've repeated it loads of times. It's a story because actually all you need to make a story is somebody doing something, if that something has meaning.

Whatever your business, it works the same way. When your customers see their own values resonate through the fabric of your organization, they see that you are like them, and that you're doing something to help achieve what you mutually want, together. It creates a story for them that they'll tell others.

So what's your brand's story? If you can't say, then it's being made up around you, whether you are aware of it or not. Because the fact is, that just by opening its doors, your business is creating stories. Start there: say there's someone watching you open your door for the first time. How many stories are there potentially in that act?

- 'Where' your business operates is a story: a hairdressers opening inside an old people's home is a great story of helping older people feel good about their appearance — but a funeral directors in the same space would be distasteful.

- The person 'who' opens your door is a story: your people either project your brand, or they undermine it.

- 'How' they open your door is a story of who is welcome: do you have a push button for the disabled? Do you have a double-handle to keep wayward toddlers from wandering out?

- Even 'what' your door looks like can create stories, either of being in line with your brand, or contradicting it.

That's four stories even before your first customer comes along, before they look at what you're selling, before you ever speak to them.

The good news is that once you've targeted your market and know what your brand values are, you can create a set of stories that brings your brand to life in such a clear way customers will connect straight away with what's important to you.

Here are some stories you want to tell over and over again:

- *Your own story as boss* How did you get here? Do you personally carry the values that your brand is about? Whatever your experience that gives you the credibility to be running your business, tell it as a story, so it will spread.

- *Your company's story* Your staff and customers all need to know what your company's story is. Fill the gap between the original idea and where you have got to for your people — take them on that journey, so they feel they're in a story that matters.

- *Stories you tell your people* When you talk to your staff, they will pick up clues about what you want to see more of, and what behaviours you're discouraging.

- *Stories your people tell customers* To the public, no one knows what's really going on in your organization better than your staff. They've got the inside knowledge. The small conversations that happen between staff and customers can create loyalty or drive customers away.

- *Stories customers tell each other* We all know word of mouth is the best kind of advertising. Stories about customer experiences are difficult to override — they are hugely believable.

- *Stories customers tell themselves* Customers are already telling themselves stories — about who they are, what they deserve and what they want. The better your company knows its customers, the more likely you are to be able to step in and create the experience they're looking for.

- *Stories that will change old ideas* Reputations can be difficult to shift, but if you can create an experience to directly contradict the old stories, gossip-mongers will lose confidence in them, and begin thinking of you in a new light, which they will spread.

Tracy Kenny has been training individuals and teams to use their stories to understand their brand and its impact for 13 years. At the time of writing she was using that experience within Aviva to expand their new brand into the insurer's extensive supply chain. Read Tracy's blog at www.tracykenny.co.uk

Day 16

YOUR BRAND NAME: HOW TO GET IT RIGHT AND HOW TO AVOID PITFALLS

There are two massive bear traps when it comes to naming or renaming a business. One is the 'does what it says on the tin' trap, and the other is the 'let's go crazy' trap. Small businesses have a terrible habit of falling into one of these.

I am frequently approached by small business owners asking me to give an opinion or advice about their brand name. People usually offer two or three choices of name and ask me to help them decide which one to go with.

Interestingly, the name choices are not usually small variations on a theme but are instead quite different in nature. They tend to fall into the following categories.

1. Does what it says on the tin names (which are generally trying to communicate something about the product or service benefit to the prospective customer).

2. Charming/wacky/weird/enigmatic names (which are trying in one way or another to make an emotional connection).

3. Straightforward labelling names (which tend to stem from the names of the founder or the origins of the business, using family names, initials and so on).

4. Made-up words (which might also be trying for some kind of emotional connection but are generally more concerned with distinctiveness and memorability, and of course online unique-ness and trademark ability).

None of these categories is any better or worse than any other. And many successful brand names cross over two or more categories. There is no single right way to name your business/brand. There is a wrong way though: and that is to be boring, to lack distinctiveness, and to be so inwardly focused that you don't trouble to imagine your brand name inside the heads and hearts, and on the tongues, of others.

Your brand name is not the be all and end all of your brand. Far from it. **A great brand experience can overcome a dodgy name. But a strong name helps**.

But how to find the name, whether you are starting from scratch or renaming a brand that already exists? My advice is always to go back to the purpose of your brand. What's it for? How will it benefit customers? What positive impact do you want to make on the world. Then think about the meaning of your brand: what do you want people to think and feel when they encounter it?

That is not to say that a name needs to express that meaning in a literal way, of course not. But going back to your purpose and meaning (your brand strategy, in fact) will give you a strong sense of whether your intended name is in alignment with what you are trying to achieve.

I'm also inclined towards short names rather than long. One word is so much easier to remember. My own brand name — Brand Strategy Guru — breaks this rule, of course, but is designed to do something else (to communicate what I do and the attitude with which I do it).

Most of all though: **settle on a name which has resonance in some way.** A name with flavour, interest, confidence and zest. But remember brand names won't do the job on their own: it's what you do as a brand that counts. That's meant to be a comfort as well as a challenge. If you've got a name which is known, be very careful about chucking it out. Focus on the brand beyond the name.

Finally, as a general rule try to stay away from initials. Because initials are a tool of convenience and not of the heart. One of my branding love-to-hates is the phenomenon of building societies and other financial institutions with perfectly workable geographical names changing themselves to meaningless collections of initials. Cheltenham & Gloucester became C&G. In my region Norwich & Peterborough has recently become N&P (underlined incidentally by one of the ugliest pieces of logo design I have ever seen).

An exception is Liverpool Victoria which recently became LV. At least in this example the brand people have made a clever (if somewhat cheesy) use of the initials to imply the word LOVE. That alone doesn't make it a great bit of branding of course, but it is at least trying to engage with its audience on some kind of emotional level.

But how do you craft a great brand name?

Brand Builder Workout

Often brand names for small businesses appear to spring out of thin air. In fact, of course that's all an illusion. What seems to be thin air is really all our experience, influences, imagination and so on. If one or more names pop up like this then that's great: but before you choose one, ask yourself the following questions.

1. Is it distinctive and different from competitors?

2. Is it 'appropriate' (will people be repelled or embarrassed by it)?

3. Is it engaging?

4. Is it informative (does it help tell your story)?

I'm not suggesting that a name has to tick all these boxes, but this can be a sensible 'sanity check'.

If you are starting with a blank sheet, with no preconceived ideas at all, then my recommendation is to use a simple grid technique (a variation on our old friend Fritz Zwicky's Morphological Analysis, but simpler). With a simple grid eight boxes wide and eight boxes deep (drawn as large as you can make it, of course) you can capture 64 words and phrases which feel to you like possible raw material for a brand name. Be bold: stick into this the grid every phrase and every word that has crossed your mind in this regard.

Then, by looking uncritically at the apparently messy collection of words, you can make links which might, just might, generate a brilliant new brand name.

It's this method which created my brand name: Brand Strategy Guru (which has been somewhat controversial, but highly effective). If you imagine me throwing words at a grid like the one I describe, trying to capture all the possible words and phrases that relate to my specialty, it's easy to picture that amongst them would have been the words: brand, strategy and guru. There were alternatives to guru of course: expert, specialist, consultant, advisor and so on. But I was trying to achieve something very specific: to communicate precisely the territory in which I was working (thus 'brand strategy') and to be absolutely definitive and authoritative (thus 'guru'). The word 'guru' also reflects the teaching/speaking/coaching aspects of my work (it means teacher, after all) and, although it's a word which is easy to mock, this actually made it more distinctive since most 'brand consultants' would steer away from it. Thus a simple grid of words gave birth to the brand.

///

A final word about naming: brand names can, of course, become valuable intellectual property in their own right, as trademarks. The subject of trademarks is a technical and complex one that is too big for this book. My advice is to find the name you think and feel is right for you, then consider whether it's important enough to have it registered as a trademark (which will depend on the size, kind and ambition of your business). If the answer is yes, then please seek specialist advice from a good trademark attorney.

REAL BRAND STORY

Voluntary Norfolk

Brian Horner, Chief Executive of Voluntary Norfolk, explains how a long-standing third sector organization rebranded to reflect its leadership role.

When an organization grows incrementally, the image it presents can fail to keep pace with what it actually does.

New services and entirely new areas of work may be developed, but unless the core brand is both broad enough to encompass a change of emphasis, or unless the brand is refreshed, public perception of the organization will remain rooted in the past.

When the box no longer matches the contents, it is time for a change.

That was the situation faced by Norwich and Norfolk Voluntary Services (NVS) a few years ago. The charity had begun life in 1969 as Norwich Organisation for Active Help (NOAH). At that time it comprized a group of young churchgoers who wanted to encourage young people to volunteer in order to help older people and disabled people.

Some 35 years later, the situation was very different. What had started out as a group of unpaid Norwich residents had developed into a registered charity with 80 staff covering the whole of Norfolk. The work had changed, too. Helping Volunteers was still a vital component of NVS's activities, but so too was working with voluntary organizations, around 300 of which had become members of NVS. Importantly, the organization's role as a representative voice for the sector was being becoming increasingly recognized by local government and other partners in the statutory sector. Yet the NVS brand did not reflect these changed priorities.

By 2006 the charity's trustees and senior managers had concluded that the NVS brand and name no longer adequately matched the scope and ambition of the organization. They decided to consider rebranding the charity and in November 2006 a major evaluation of the NVS brand was undertaken, led by Simon Middleton. It involved both trustees and the charity's staff whose clearly expressed preference was for a more dynamic look that gave a better idea of the services and expertise on offer.

It was considered that the name Norwich and Norfolk Voluntary Services was cumbersome when given in full, and misleading when broken down. It was also felt that the logo and principle seemed rather underpowered: what was needed was something altogether bolder.

There were a number of factors affecting the timing of a full or partial rebrand. These included:

- An impending move and change of premises. Would it be potentially advantageous or disadvantageous to unveil a new brand and the new location at the same time?

- The sector's perception of NVS, and NVS's perception of its place within the sector, Norfolk, and the Eastern Region as a whole. The organization would have to decide whether it was content to work only within Norfolk or whether progression to a regional/national role was likely.

Taking these factors into account, the charity's trustees were presented with three options. The first was maintaining the status quo; the second was refreshing the existing brand NVS brand by changing the name and look but trying to maintain perceived strengths and maintain continuity; the third was fully re-branding to create a new, dynamic identity that matched the scope and ambition of the organization.

Maintaining the status quo was not viable, while refreshing the existing brand was seen as a slightly half-hearted move that would provide no long-term solution to the problem. So it was decided to fully rebrand.

Simon and his designer Scott Poulson were briefed to create something that really stood out when compared to other third-sector organizations, whether local or national, and to find a name that was shorter than Norwich and Norfolk Voluntary Services. It needed to be one that was easily remembered and that would not need to be reduced to an acronym.

From a range of name options *Voluntary Norfolk* best indicated the scope of the charity and the range of activities undertaken.

A bold typographic logo design was created in four warm, welcoming colours (magenta, pink, purple and orange) which was bright and contemporary looking with a slightly Pop Art/Music Hall poster feel that seemed to acknowledge the lineage of the organization.

In order to provide some continuity with the old NVS brand and to provide an instant explanation of the charity's main areas of responsibility, the strapline 'Supporting Volunteers and Voluntary Organizations' was retained from the old NVS logo and ran beneath the main title.

The new brand and the new offices were both launched on 17 March 2008. There were a few grumbles about the change of look, but with the old strapline present to provide reassurance that the charity had not forgotten its core principles, the new identity was quickly accepted by the sector.

A couple of years on from the launch it is clear that we made the right choice when we went with Simon's suggestion to adopt an identity that was bold, innovative and radically different from the vast majority of charities in the sector. Now, at last, the box matches its contents.

Day 17

CRAFTING THE INTERNAL BRAND POSITIONING STATEMENT

A phrase like 'positioning statement' might sound a bit technical from the off (a bit 'marketing speak' perhaps). But despite its rather uninspiring name, a positioning statement plays a very valuable role in building your brand.

Writing one is not that tricky to do properly either, as long as you understand what it is, what it's for, and how it works. *Positioning statement* is just a formal name for a sentence or short paragraph which really sums up what your brand is about and where it stands in the world and the market place (its position).

A positioning statement has several uses, and all of them are valuable to you.

- It clearly explains what the brand is about, for your staff (including new recruits and those who've been with you from the start), your backers, the media, and your bank manager.

- It reminds you what your brand is meant to be about, which is very handy when you're under stress, losing your nerve or thinking of developing something new.

- Although it is primarily for 'internal' use, a good positioning statement also gives a 'ready to use' piece of text for press releases and a host of other places where you might need to describe your brand without having to invent something every time.

So that's what a positioning statement is for, but what is it exactly? Perhaps the best definition that I've come across explains it something like this:

A positioning statement paints a picture of the brand's ambition and its vision in three ways:

- by defining what 'success' means for the brand;

- by laying down the 'rules' of how success will be achieved;

●   by explaining how customers 'benefit' from that success.

Blimey, that still sounds all techno-marketing doesn't it? But let's look closer.

'Success' just means describing what your brand is trying to achieve.

'Rules' just means how you are going to go about doing that.

'Benefit' just means describing how your customers are going to be better off, happier, more fulfilled, or satisfied by all your efforts.

By way of example, this is the positioning statement I wrote before launching Brand Strategy Guru:

"Brand Strategy Guru aims to be the best-known independent brand strategy advisor in the UK, giving accessible brand advice (through consultancy, workshops, conference speaking, writing and broadcasting), so that all kinds of non-marketing specialist people can learn to use the power of branding for their businesses."

'Success' for my brand means becoming the best-known independent brand strategy advisor in the UK.

'Rules' in my case means: giving accessible brand advice (through consultancy, workshops, conference speaking, writing and broadcasting).

'Benefits' to customers are: that all kinds of non-marketing specialist people can learn to use the power of branding for their businesses.

Before we move on to you writing your own positioning statement (oh yes, you knew that was coming, didn't you?), a couple of other things to notice.

1. Keep it short and fairly simple. Positioning statements don't tell all the ins and outs of how the company works and all its different products and services. They tell a big story in a very few words.

2. Don't be so detailed as to be inflexible. You really don't want a positioning statement that you have to alter every time you launch a new product. Keep it flexible and strong, not brittle.

3. Stay clear and specific. Avoid being too grandiose or too broad in scope.

Brand Builder Workout

We've established what a positioning statement is for and how to construct one. Now it's your turn. Perhaps the easiest way to do this is in by using the three elements of success, rules and customer benefits.

So…

Success: Describe here what success looks like for your brand. You can think of it in geographical terms, or size, or reputation.

Rules: Describe here how you will achieve that success, by describing what you are going to provide in terms of products, services, expertise, etc.. Remember not to get too detailed.

Benefits: Describe here how your customers' lives will be enhanced by what you do.

Now the crafting bit. Once you are happy with your three elements you need to shape them into a sentence or two which you feel is authentic, convincing and genuinely descriptive of what your brand is trying to achieve.

Write it down here:

Live with it. Say it out loud. Try to look at it from the perspective of one of your junior staff, or your bank manager, or a journalist. Does it clarify what your brand is about?

Don't worry if it seems ambitious. Don't worry if you haven't achieved it yet. The question is whether it is sufficiently ambitious and yet also sufficiently grounded to be achievable. Now test it with your team, or with someone you trust if you don't have a team. Do they understand it?

When you're happy that it is just right then type it out, print it and stick on your wall for a while. Tweak it if necessary over a few days. In time it will 'settle' and once it has reached that state it is ready to use.

Day 18

SHAPING THE EXTERNAL BRAND POSITIONING LINE

In the previous chapter we looked at the 'positioning statement', the focus of which is largely internal: in other words, it acts as a guide for you and your team about the core purpose of your brand and organization. In this chapter, by contrast, we look outwards, towards your customers and potential customers, with the 'positioning line'.

Let's clear up something right from the start: you may not need a positioning line. I haven't got one (I have used them effectively in other businesses but don't do so with my current brand, Brand Strategy Guru). Having said that, I recommend that you work through this chapter before you decide whether your brand will or won't benefit from a positioning line.

But what exactly is a positioning line? It frequently gets referred to as a 'strapline' or even simply as a slogan. A positioning line is, at its simplest, the short phrase or set of words that appears alongside (or, more often than not, underneath) a brand's logo or name.

For example:

John Lewis: Never Knowingly Undersold

Tesco: Every Little Helps

Nike: Just Do It

Orange: The Future's Bright

O2: We're better connected

Budweiser: King Of Beers

AUDI: Vorsprung Durch Technik

McDonald's: I'm lovin' it

And so on. Positioning lines are everywhere. Our job here is to decide whether or not a line will make a contribution to your efforts to build your brand, and if so, how to make one.

Let's deal with the first question first. My rule of thumb is that a very good strapline can be a real asset, and a hardworking one into the bargain, in the following circumstances:

1. You are operating in a crowded marketplace in which a 'line' can help you to differentiate yourself from your competitors.

2. You have a strong reputation but you want to add some reassurance or another nuance to your brand.

3. Your business needs a bit of quick explanation in some way, to help people understand what's on offer.

4. Your brand name is a bit dry and functional, in which case a line can help give some emotional flavour or punch.

5. Your brand name is quite abstract in which case a line can help deliver some useful information.

6. Your brand name is abstract and/or emotionally based rather than functional, but you want to add even more emotion.

7. Your brand name has been around for a while but you want to change your brand 'meaning', in which case a new line can help to reposition you.

8. You want to encourage people (inside and outside the organization) to enthusiastically gather around some kind of campaign, in which case a line can be a powerful distillation of your message.

These eight scenarios are by no means mutually exclusive: it is perfectly possible for them to overlap. But let's have a look at just a few examples to illustrate the point.

Never Knowingly Undersold

John Lewis is famous (as we've explored earlier in this book) for quality, service, value and partnership rather than for price. In fact most JL shoppers are not going there for low prices at all. Nevertheless, this longstanding positioning line reassures these customers that, whilst they may not be terribly price-sensitive, their trusted store will not exploit their trust by inflating their prices.

The Future's Bright

When Orange launched, the line was longer, reading The Future's Bright, The Future's Orange. Then it was a radical approach that must take some credit for the rapid establishment of Orange as a highly distinctive brand in its sector. The name was already abstract, but bravely, rather than try to 'explain' it the brand's line adds a powerful emotion: optimism. Proof, if proof were needed that emotions make brands. Orange has become less interesting in recent years by focusing on tariffs rather than emotion, but the point still stands.

We Are Macmillan

This is one example of a recent trend in positioning lines: in which the name of the brand and the line are wrapped up together. Cancer charity Macmillan has given itself a confident and action-oriented brand meaning through the use of this hybrid name line.

Vorsprung Durch Technik

This classic line, from AUDI of course, is interesting in a number of ways, most notably because it's in German and most English-speaking people don't know what it means. It means (roughly) 'forward through technology', but it doesn't actually matter because it just sounds strong and Teutonic and efficient and impressive in an engineering sort of way, which is precisely in line with AUDI's intentions as a brand. It is also very old, having originally been a slogan on a factory wall (a kind of internal brand statement), so it has a kind of authenticity and durability which thousands of other brands strive for and fail to achieve.

A Higgledy-Piggledy World Of Pleasure

This is from Norfolk café-restaurant Byfords. No mention of tea, cakes or any other functional elements here. Pure emotion delivered with charm and wit.

If none of the eight scenarios above apply to you then I'm not convinced that a positioning line will be massively helpful to you, but if any of them do, then how you go about writing one?

There are some simple rules.

1. Keep it short. It's a slogan, not an essay. I can't think of a well-known strapline of more than six words, and most of them are three or four.

2. A line should either 'evoke' an emotional response or deliver explanatory information, not both. The choice of which way to go depends of your circumstance (refer back to the eight scenarios above).

3. Use simple language, unless you specifically and deliberately want to create an effect by using unusual words.

4. A strapline is not a motto: at all costs avoid Latin, avoid quotations, and avoid any kind of pomposity.

5. Try to write a line that can be substantiated (i.e. one that will be proven by experiencing the brand). Audi's line, along with Byford's and John Lewis's, are all true and 'specific' to them.

For this reason (and a million others) please do not **ever** use 'simply the best' or any other words like these.

6. Please try to avoid being too 'puntastic'. I don't hate puns *per se* but I think they are dangerous in straplines. They just look like they're working too hard. O2's *We're better connected* is a case in point. We all get the double meaning, but there is something intrinsically smug and non-communicative about double meanings like this. My advice: avoid them.

7. Make every word count. As far as possible, avoid too many non-working words like 'the', 'and', 'in', etc.

8. Write ten different lines before you choose one.

9. Test your favourites on other people before you make a final decision.

10. Have at least one other person check the line carefully for grammar and spelling. I have seen too many apostrophes in the wrong place and misspellings to take this for granted. There is a town not far from me in which an office supplies shop proudly proclaims on a huge (professionally produced) fascia board that it is the district's 'finest stationary supplier'. Staggeringly, I have seen another business in the area offering 'Freshly caught fihs and chips'. Honestly.

Brand Builder Workout

There are two parts to today's workout. First, looking at other brands' positioning lines. Second, drafting your own.

Take a walk around your nearest shopping centre, browse a little while on the internet, and leaf through a few newspapers and magazines. Make a note here of 10 positioning lines which you think work effectively, either by delivering important information or by evoking an emotional response. Also make a list of 10 lines which you think don't cut the mustard, and make a brief note of why they fail.

10 effective *informational* straplines

- _____

- _____

- _____

- _____

- _____

- _____

- _____

- _____

- _____

- _____

10 effective *emotional* straplines

- _____

- _____

- _____

- _____

- _____

- _____

- _____

- _____

- _____

- _____

10 straplines which don't work

- --

- --

- --

- --

- --

- --

- --

- --

- --

- --

Now, based on your research into other brands' lines, and the 10 simple rules above, try to write some possible lines for yourself. It can be immensely helpful to carry around a scrap of paper or a notebook for a few days with this challenge in the back of your mind. In my experience of writing brand positioning lines, the really good ones invariably pop into your head when you are least expecting it (providing that you have primed your brain with the challenge – rather wonderfully our brains get on with this kind of creative processing activity while we're busy doing something else).

That's not to say that a hardcore scribbling session won't help. Put an hour aside to really work at this, and the combination of hard graft and subconscious processing will produce a killer result (as long as you remember my simple rules).

10 strapline ideas for your brand

- --

- --

- --

- --

- --

- --

- --

- --

- --

- --

REAL BRAND STORY

Anthony Nolan

David Knights, Director of Marketing and Communications at Anthony Nolan, explains how a charity much-loved by an older generation addressed the need to reinvent itself for a younger and more diverse audience.

At a little over 35 years old, The Anthony Nolan Trust was a very effective charity. It had found the last hope for survival for a vast number of children and adults: patients who were suffering from leukaemia or similar potentially fatal conditions. The Anthony Nolan Trust runs the UK's largest and most successful bone marrow register. The volunteers who have joined this register can go on to donate their bone marrow if their tissue type matches that of a patient anywhere in the world. In 2008, the charity had its most successful year ever by providing a record number of patients, over 750, with their chance of life.

Despite its pre-eminent position The Anthony Nolan Trust noted that it had a real long-term problem. Its traditional supporters (including those who personally remembered Shirley Nolan's campaign on behalf of her son Anthony), were growing older whilst the target market of 18–30 year olds were barely aware of the charity's existence, let alone that they were critically vital to the growth of the lifesaving bone marrow register.

Following market research a few years ago, the charity gave itself a facelift; basically tidying up its logo with a more assertive colour and strapline because it needed to diminish its undue modesty. Since that time, The Anthony Nolan Trust has embarked on an ambitious strategy for growth. The directors recognized that they needed to carry out a full-scale rebrand this time; not just another change in its visual identity. More recent market research revealed that the highly-prized younger target audience remained largely unaware of the charity. On top of that, The Anthony Nolan Trust clearly understood that it couldn't take for granted the loyalty of its current supporters. No charity can.

Simon was commissioned to guide the charity's management through a total rebrand. Simon worked closely with my team and with the full support of the Chief Executive. He was deeply involved in a number of different stages of the rebrand. Using the results of the existing market research, for example, Simon held telephone discussions with more supporters and then led staff workshops in which he teased out the foundations of the charity's brand values.

His recommendations were accepted by the senior management team and trustees. He proposed changes in three main areas: revision of the charity's public name; defining and living out a set of core values; and changing the ways in which the charity presented itself to its audiences.

The charity had been conservative and modest, but the time was ripe for a more fundamental shift in gear. There was a move to develop more ambitious plans for growth. The senior management team and then the trustees accepted Simon's recommendations: a shortening of the charity's name to Anthony Nolan, identifying the brand values as focused, innovative and trusted, and creating a completely new visual look and tone of voice.

Following presentations from brand agencies, the Marketing & Communications team drew up a shortlist of options for the charity's new look. Simon managed further consultation with the staff to test the possible designs against the brand values. The preferred designs were reworked and Simon ran focus groups amongst supporters and members of the general public who were unaware of the charity to highlight any remaining issues around the more popular designs. The results led to a specific new look being presented to the senior management team and, ultimately, the trustees as the new brand identity.

Day 19

NURTURING YOUR
GREATEST RESOURCE: YOU

Building a business is tough enough to put most people off. And the stats are alarming. If you want my advice, don't even go near the stats. And if building a business is tough then building a brand, in some sense at least, is an even greater challenge. I never promised you it would be easy.

Actually, as I hope this book is demonstrating convincingly, the individual steps required are not that difficult, complex or expensive. What they are, though, is demanding of your intellect, your emotions, your sustained effort, and in a sense your soul.

This chapter is a kind of time-out to think about what it means to make a brand out of nothing and why it sometimes seems like a very steep uphill struggle.

Since we're really talking about small brands in this book, it is a safe assumption that you are the driving force behind the business and the brand. And if not, then you are the appointed 'brand champion': someone who is trusted to nurture the brand and help it move forward with energy and vision. Whichever one you are you will face many of the same ups and downs, triumphs and disappointments.

Let's deal first with triumphs. In my little office I have a small brass handbell with a wooden handle. It was bought for me from a car boot sale by a colleague at a company that I used to run with a partner. And it was bought as a replacement for a previous bell which I had worn out through over use! What's the bell for? Simple. The bell is used to celebrate the small (or large) triumphs that the business encounters.

There's a simple rule. If it's good news of a 'definite' kind, the bell rings and the household celebrates. It might be an engagement to speak at a conference. It might be some good media coverage. It might be a new client or a major new project. It actually doesn't matter whether it's a large triumph or a small one: I believe that it's important to celebrate them all. The big ones (the client wins, the major bookings) get a little extra treatment: a bottle of champagne gets popped or an impromptu dinner out is arranged. But the small stuff still gets the bellringing.

And this celebration is so important for one very simple reason. Because building a brand can include many, many days of not much coming back to you from the great beyond. Brand building for small businesses can be lonely stuff. You issue a press release and apparently nothing happens. You send out a proposal to an apparently enthusiastic prospective customer, following a really positive and optimistic meeting, and nothing happens. You have a **huge** project all signed-up with a **huge** client (a project which will pay your bills and your salary for the next six months at least): then the client announces **huge** losses and the project is cancelled. All of these have happened to me more than once. Some of them happen quite a lot. Oh there'll be plenty of disappointments along the way, so I'm absolutely strict about the celebration rule. If it's positive: celebrate it.

We all know Kipling's much-quoted line about triumph and disaster and how we should treat each of those 'imposters' just the same. He's right in a sense, of course, and it's important not to get the triumphs out of proportion. But believe me, the 'disasters' will occupy your mind aplenty when they arrive, so it's actually important (if we are to treat them just the same) to make sure we dwell on the triumphs for a little while too. You'd be surprised how many entrepreneurs are afraid to celebrate success. I've met more than one highly successful business owner who was deeply anxious about celebration, for fear that it would somehow spook the whole enterprise. It's quite right to avoid hubris (pride coming before a fall and all that), but that really must not prevent you from celebrating. Remember, it's not just you who needs that uplift: it's your team, and your family (the long-suffering and supportive partner is top of the list of people deserving a sign of well-deserved success).

You don't have to have a bell. You don't have to have champagne. Celebrate your way. But do celebrate. And then remember it in some way. Make a note in your diary or something. You'll need it later in the tough bits.

Once you've done celebrating it's worth looking at the success, of whatever kind or degree, and thinking about why and how it came about. Try to analyze it a bit. Where did it all go right? If you can find one or two distinguishing characteristics of this particular success you might be able to increase the chances of it happening again. It is folk wisdom that we learn from our mistakes (or at least that we should do). But it's just as important (and I think much less common) for us to actually learn from our successes.

A small example: I was hired recently to appear in a TV programme about British seaside businesses. I'm not the star of the show, but a kind of 'advisor' to the presenter who is himself a hugely successful and very well-known entrepreneur. I got this strange little gig through a chain of coincidences, all stemming from my agreeing to do some *pro bono* work for a small seaside community not far from where I live. In fact, that's not where it started. In fact, a small business owner in the little seaside resort (Hemsby in Norfolk) found me on a search engine while looking for somebody to give the resort some brand advice. I met the Hemsby traders, liked them and their commitment to the 'brand' of Hemsby, and agreed to do some work for them voluntarily. We made a bit of noise about the resort in the media. That in turn was noticed by a TV production company who had just won a commission to make a series about seaside towns. They found me via one of the Hemsby traders.

So what are the lessons in this little success?

First, that *pro bono* work frequently turns out (whilst it is never guaranteed to do so) to be hugely valuable to the giver. It just seems to be that favours beget good outcomes. I'm not remotely 'mystical' about this, and I'm a determined opponent of all that nonsense about 'ask the universe for something and you will be rewarded'. Let's keep our feet on the ground and our brains in the real world, eh? However, having said that, there are much more mundane reasons why this stuff works. You do something positive and people talk about it (and by talk I include the media, online, in actual conversation etc.). Then more people talk about it. Then somebody hears about it. And the important thing is not that you did something on a voluntary basis. The important thing is that you acted in some way that had a positive impact, no matter how small.

Second, that everything is connected. There really aren't that many occasions when an action takes place in isolation. On this occasion something positive tumbled along down the chain and gave me a terrific opportunity, which I am certain will lead to other good things. But heed the warning in this story too. What of all the occasions when I might have (indeed actually have) turned down an invitation like the one from Hemsby? The missed opportunities about which we shall never know because we didn't allow them to happen. And, just as important if not more so, what of the times when I haven't served my clients or my contacts well. If positive news travels fast and far, we all know it has nothing like the pace and stamina of bad news.

Third, that having a big-picture brand strategy is terribly important. It is a key part of my brand strategy to develop a reputation as an expert in my field (which happens to be 'brand strategy', but don't let that throw you: it's just as applicable to a retailer or a tiler or a pork-pie maker). And what does a reputation for expertise demand, first and foremost? It demands that you exercise that expertise, widely and frequently. If Hemsby traders had asked me to look at their accounts I would have declined because I'm not an account-ant. And if they had been in Cornwall I would have had to say no because of geography. Because geography means travel costs, and we had established there was no money. But what they asked was bang on the nail of my strategy, and achievable because we are geo-graphically close. There was, therefore, a pretty good chance that the project was achievable and that the outcome would be positive although, of course, I could not anticipate the specifics or even the nature of that outcome. In other words it wasn't a blind choice. It was an educated hunch. To be honest, educated hunches are fre-quently the best you've got. They usually work, too; but only when you genuinely combine 'educated' (facts and insights) with 'hunch' (your best instincts, not your reckless dreams).

The other of Kipling's imposters, and perhaps the more challenging to deal with, is failure. You will, I guarantee, meet disappointments frequently and disasters occasionally. More often, and perhaps more draining and potentially more threatening, because we don't pre-pare ourselves for them, are the periods which can only be described as those when there is not much happening.

Not much happening is a bad sensation for the brand champion and it can drain your morale faster than a bath with no plug. Let's look at this phenomenon first. You probably already know the scenario. You've been working terribly hard at your product or your service, or your marketing, or your networking, at something, anyway. It feels like you are making great efforts but where are the results? No greater number of people are coming through the door or calling up or visiting your website. Sales might be ticking along. You're not in imminent danger of the business collapsing, but it's all just a bit flat. This is a dangerous time. This is the time where people throw their brand strategies (if they have them) out of the window. Or more likely they just leave them lying in the metaphorical and dusty bot-tom drawer of the office desk. But the danger isn't just in the neglect of your carefully created strategy. The real threat comes in what you might find yourself doing instead of following the strategy.

This is the time when you chase after shiny things, distractions and less-than-half-baked ideas which suddenly seem so much more appealing and promising than your current business or brand. Watch out for this urge, because the distractions will come as surely as night follows day. They will flood in through your email inbox. They will come on the phone. They will pop up in every magazine that you read as a distraction from what you should be concentrating on. It's not that these distractions aren't there at other times. It's just that you don't notice them (or rather you more easily dismiss them) when you are feeling strong and focused. But when your guard is down, when you're in the not-much-happening place, you will be tempted to go running after them.

There is only one cure for the 'not-much-happening blues' and that is to make something happen. Go back to your strategy. Remind yourself why you're doing this. Remind yourself of your 'purpose' and refocus on all the elements that you know need your continued attention. This is where you must take the long view (and this is where your 'soul' comes into it) and think beyond the immediate slough of despond. And, to be blunt, it is the ability to do that which will separate you from the wannabe brand-makers who don't actually make it. It's got nothing to do with 'asking the universe' and everything to do with summoning the energy to follow the strategy you have so carefully constructed.

What about the real failures, though? The ones that seem to threaten to undermine everything you thought you were creating as a brand and a business? I've had my fair share of these. They are pretty devastating when they happen. In my trade (which you can broadly call 'marketing'), they can sometimes come in the shape of a client refusing to pay a bill, or trying to pay less, because they say you have not delivered on what you promised. The only sensible strategy here has three elements.

1. Apologise to the client for their dissatisfaction. No matter what the rights and wrongs of the situation, you have to do that first. It hurts sometimes, but it's pretty much rule one of customer service. As the saying goes, the customer may not always be right, but they are always the customer.

2. Examine how you got to this uncomfortable place. That can often take a bit of unpicking, but it's worth doing, not to be morbid but in order to find out how it might be avoided in future. Now it might turn out to be all your fault. More often, it turns out to be an uncomfortable mixture of your fault and the customer's fault. In the marketing business it so often seems to be a matter of unrealistic customer expectations (which should have been better managed by the business). Whatever the reasons turn out to be, keep them to yourself and your team.

3. Take ameliorative action with the customer. No matter how you feel about the injustice of it (and you may have to soothe some wounded pride amongst your team) it's at this point where you have to overcompensate to the customer. Remember, the idea is to leave them with a a very positive feeling about your brand. And it's worth overcompensating in order to achieve that. Never ever let pride and a misplaced sense of justice stand in the way of this. Otherwise you are damaging your brand. It's that simple.

So you've followed those steps and your customer is placated and will probably tell others that you are marvellous (because you acted for the brand, not for your hurt feelings), but you are left feeling absolutely dreadful .You wonder if all your effort is worth it. You wonder if you will ever get your staff to understand the brand and how to treat customers. You wonder if you're up to this. If you're in the business of offering advice, as I am, then these sorts of incidents can provoke a real existential crisis. Am I good enough? Am I a fraud? If all my clients don't think I'm brilliant all the time then how can I call myself an expert? If you've experienced this wracking self-doubt then I don't need to emphasize how unpleasant and how potentially dangerous it is. If you haven't experienced it, then remember this chapter. Because you're going to experience it at some point. It may not come from a problem with a customer. It may come from a lack of customers. Or a lack of sales. Or a staff problem. It could come from anywhere. It will come, though.

There are no prizes for guessing what I believe to be the cure. That's right: go back to the strategy. That's why this book, in the long term as well as the short, will be so important to you. Because when all else fails you'll have a strategy. You will be able to remind yourself what your brand 'is for'. And you'll also be able to remind yourself that the truth about brand and branding is that success does not demand human perfection, or even human extraordinariness. What it demands is the application of certain principles and practices. And they are all here in this book.

So by all means allow yourself to feel miserable and grumpy. No-one can tell you your emotions aren't valid. **Brands are all about emotion. But don't let those emotions drag you down. Go back to the strategy**. Remind yourself that you don't have to be perfect. Nobody is. Remind yourself why you believed in this business before. And if necessary remind your team, too.

Whilst we're dealing with all things downbeat about owning and building a brand, I want to address another truth about the endeavour (that I regard as self-evident but which, to my puzzlement, many people seem to think can be avoided). And this truth is that there is real risk, financial as well as psychological, in setting out on this road. To be absolutely honest, in my time I've tried to talk a few people out of setting up businesses. It always feels uncomfortable at the time. I hate being a pessimist (I'm a card-carrying optimist by nature, but I've learned to control it), but some folk go into this entrepreneurship thing with ideas that are unrealistic and dreams that are fragile. And success depends on the opposite: ideas that are realistic coupled with dreams that are as tough as old boots. **Running a business and building a brand are not activities for the easily hurt.**

So, there is risk. You may be lucky. You may make money fast and you may make it consistently. It can happen. You might be one of those with the seemingly magic touch. In which case you're probably not reading this book anyway. But for the rest of us risk is inevitable. My advice on this is simple and two-fold. It also comes with a caveat, and the caveat is to take financial advice from someone qualified to give it to you. Which frankly isn't me, but the following are what I believe to be sensible guidelines, and they are presented here together with their unavoidable implications (though some people do try to avoid them).

Guideline One: You cannot start a business or build a brand half-heartedly. Not a proper business anyway. Not a business that will inspire you and others. Not a brand that you can really be proud of. And the need to be wholehearted doesn't just imply that you will put in time and effort (in such quantities as most people will find hard to imagine). It also means that you will have to risk money. This book will save you money, I hope, because it will save you spending money unnecessarily or through ignorance. But you will have to spend money at some point. And when you do, spend it cheerfully as well as wisely. Things not to try to do on the cheap include: commissioning design, paying staff, ensuring superb customer service. There are many others. And you will have to pay out for them. And every pound you spend is a pound risked. That's the fact. Unavoidable. If you are not comfortable with carrying around a degree of risk then this is not the journey for you.

Guideline Two: Do not risk more than you can afford to lose. It's the corollary of Guideline One. And it's important to clarify. Risk is unavoidable and important. In some senses it is not only positive but a key part of the endeavour of enterprise. But too large a risk is just that: too large. In my business I have risked substantial amounts of money. I have risked becoming poor if it goes wrong, which it has sometimes threatened to do. I have risked reputation and I have risked real financial difficulty on a substantial scale. But I have never risked the home that my family live in. For me that is too much. Others will have different thresholds. It's not for me to decide your threshold: but you need to decide. Decide what you can and cannot risk, and don't forget where the boundary lies between the two.

There are two other truths about building a brand and a business that I think all entrepreneurs need to think about and find a position on. The first is the illusion that making money is the be all and end all. To be blunt, if that is your belief then there may well be more reliable ways to make money than trying to build a brand. There isn't room to go into those options here: suffice to say that making a brand has more rewards than just money. Maybe, for instance, you'd be better off staying in your high salary corporate job if you've worked hard enough and been lucky enough to secure one. Having said that, I am always very wary of those people who claim that money doesn't matter to them at all. Money is not the only measure of a good brand. But it is a measure. And if your brand consistently fails to make money, month in, month out, year after year then it isn't a business, it's a hobby. Nothing wrong with that. But you need to be honest with yourself about what you are doing and why. Because there have to be better hobbies than building a brand which nobody wants to pay for.

You can tell from this somewhat reflective chapter what I mean when I say that building a brand is about using our humanity. That's what makes it such a great adventure, and why your greatest asset will always be you, yourself. Look after it.

Day 20

Do-it-Yourself Media Relations

In this chapter you'll learn why PR is so extraordinarily important to the process of building a brand, and therefore why you absolutely have to be active in this area, even if you do nothing else that could be described as marketing.

First, a few definitions, so we're all clear what we're talking about when we talk about PR.

Brand: well, you know this by now, but just for the record, your 'brand' is everything that your customers think, feel, hear, see, read, believe, suspect, hope and wish about you, your company, your product or your service. Brand is an output (it's not something you do, it's something that exists).

Branding: is an input, something you do. In short, branding is everything you do to nurture a positive and strong brand. It's not the same as marketing.

Marketing: is an umbrella term for the whole process of taking your product, service or business to market. It's big and complex and it includes things like research at the front end of the process, as well as product pricing and a host of other elements from promotions to advertising, etc., etc. Lots of people think that branding is a part of this great big marketing process. I don't. I think brand and branding are different to marketing and have much more significance than used to be the case. Because, as you've heard me say several times, brand and branding are about meaning rather than process. Most aspects of marketing are inputs: stuff you do. And in the main you are in control of those inputs: though almost never the outputs.

Advertising: is an activity in which you buy some media space (space in a newspaper or magazine, or on TV or the cinema, or on a website or a poster/billboard) and fill that space with your message.

You're completely in control of the input. In other words you can (within some legal limits) say pretty much what you like. You can be clever and creative or direct and informative. Whatever you fancy. But you're not in control of the output (what people think and feel).

We need to clarify these few things in order to put PR in context. PR is simply short for 'public relations'. But what does that mean? In the broadest sense, public relations is concerned with the relationship between a company/product/service (or an individual person) and their 'public' (in other words, anybody they need to have a relationship of some kind with). The broad term of PR can mean anything from getting your political message across on Newsnight to putting up a polite sign outside your office to apologize for inconvenience caused by building work, to issuing a press release about a new contract or appointment. PR can also embrace specialized areas like crisis management.

But for our purposes here we're going to focus on the most common interpretation of PR, because it's the one that will actually help you to build your brand and the one which you can quickly learn to put into action effectively. It's technically called 'media relations' (meaning it's about your relationships with the press, TV/radio and other media). Journalists and editors, in other words.

By far the vast majority of PR activity going on at any moment is actually media relations. But I call it PR and I think we can too. PR has three highly distinguishing characteristics compared to almost anything else you do in relation to your brand.

First: it's free (hurrah!).

Second: you're not only not in control of the output, but you're not really in complete control of the input either (boooo!).

Third: when PR succeeds it really succeeds because (as plenty of research proves) people are much more inclined to believe what they read in a press article or hear on the news than they are to believe what they see or watch in an ad or a TV commercial (hurrah!). Notwithstanding the fact that many of us have a healthy caution about the veracity of popular newspapers, we still trust them more than we trust advertising (which doesn't mean that advertising doesn't work; but that's another story and indeed another chapter).

I'll explain. PR is free because you don't have to pay journalists and editors to use your press releases (I'll come back to press releases). This is jolly good, and it's one of the beautiful things about PR that makes it such a powerful tool for the small brand-builder. That's not really to say that you won't have to spend some money when you do PR. For example, you'll want to have good photographs to send with your press release, won't you? And you'll also want and need to apply some time to doing PR properly, and time, as we all know, is money. But the simple truth remains that you don't have to 'buy the space', which makes PR completely different from advertising.

It's this very advantage of being free that also carries the downside of not being in control of the input. Of course you're in control of what you say in a press release. But you're not in control of whether said press release gets used by the journalist or passed for publication by the editor. Neither are you in control of what the journalist or editor does by way of rewriting, cutting or otherwise altering the release that you have so carefully crafted.

That, in a nutshell, is the devil's pact of PR. You don't pay for it, but there are no guarantees of any kind, at all, ever. But the irony of this pact is that this is precisely what makes PR so effective as a brand-building tool; once your press release has managed to cross the no-man's-land of the editorial process and finally made its way wounded and shell-shocked but still more or less in one piece into the newspaper or the news broadcast or onto the website, it will be treated by the reader with the subconscious respect with which we treat all news. We make the general assumption that it is in all probability more or less accurate and more or less fair.

So PR is a curious process that might seem like terribly hard work with little guarantee of result. Correction. It is moderately hard work with no guarantee at all of result; but when you do get a result it can be of immense value to your brand, out of all proportion to the effort involved, and hugely out of proportion to the cost involved. So, PR is good for you. And this is how you do it.

First rule of DIY-PR is to treat journalists (whether reporters, feature writers, columnists, editors, freelancers, whatever) with respect, but not with fear. Journalists are professionals like any others. They are using real skills and well-honed instincts to do a really professional job of bringing news, information and ideas to their readers, viewers and listeners. In doing this they rely in part on PR people (which now includes you) bringing them good quality and appropriate material. Sometimes that material constitutes the raw facts about something of significance that has just happened. This is called hard news, and the important word in this description is 'significance'. A national newspaper will generally see as significant only things which have a national or international relevance. A local radio station will be much more open to news about a local news event. But journalists don't live by hard news alone. The media is filled with long features on every kind of topic, with interviews, with gossip, with ideas and with debate. And journalists can't find all this material on their own. They absolutely rely on and welcome contributions from PRs like you.

The point is that, whilst your brand is unlikely to be creating internationally important hard news, virtually every other kind of editorial opportunity is open to you *provided* you consider the needs of the journalist above all else. So never be afraid of journalists. They want to hear from you. But equally, respect them, don't waste their time. Instead give them the good stuff.

Journalists like what they sometimes refer to as 'packages'. In other words they like to have things presented to them in a form that is as readily usable as possible. A typical package might include:

- an introductory/covering note;

- a press release (the news bit);

- some background information (extra stuff they can use or refer to if they wish but which isn't crucial to the story);

- a choice of very good photographs which they won't be embarrassed showing to their picture editor;

- all the contact details they need to follow up the story.

Let's take each of these is in turn. None of them are difficult. And if you can put all these together then you've got the makings of your first press release and it's a pattern you can repeat over and over.

It's important to say here that virtually all PR (at least the part of PR that is about sending material to people) is now done by email and not by post or by hand delivery. Most journalists just won't look at a press release that arrives as hard copy. It's just got to be email. That's it. And whenever possible, you should send your email to a named person, and therefore to an individual email address. They're not that difficult to come by. If you want the cookery editor of a national magazine you can generally phone up the magazine (details are on the website if you search) and ask for the address. You might be asked to explain who you are and why you need the address, but that's fine; consider it good practice for when you speak to the journalist.

Of course, it's common courtesy to introduce yourself. But more than that, if you can give a journalist a one liner in the covering email about why you think that your press release will be of interest, then you're much more likely to get their attention. Don't over-promise and avoid superlatives and hyperbole. Your story is unlikely to be the most exciting thing they've read in the last hour, let alone all day or all year, so don't get carried away. Just tell them enough to whet their appetite. Like all branding activity, be different (i.e. not like everyone else), be compelling, but also be authentic (real, true, honest).

This core of your package is the press release itself. It involves writing. But don't let it freak you out if you don't think you're a writer. Instead just focus on what you're trying to do, which is to deliver an interesting and coherent message to somebody. It helps to break it into bits, and to ask questions as you go, like this:

1. What is the most important 'single' thing that you want to communicate? That's your headline. And remember your headline shouldn't be punning or clever: it should sum up the story. Clever–clever headlines, I'm sorry to say, are the province of the newspaper subeditors. Your job is to lead the journalist into your story.

2. If the journalist was only going to read 30 words what would you want them to be? That's your opening paragraph. The whole story in a sentence or two. To do this you have to strip it down to the bare essentials. Use this checklist if it helps:

    ● What's happened or is going to happen?

    ● Who is making it happen or to whom is it happening?

    ● Where and when did it (or will it) happen?

    ● Who did this happening have an effect on and how?

    ● Why is it important (what's the wider impact)?

    ● What do people think or feel about this thing that's happened?

3. Now you've got the essentials across, what additional facts do you need to give about each element? These are your next paragraphs. There is no real rule about the order in which you tackle things, but I always try to go in the order as above: from what's happening through to what people think about it.

It's important sometimes to give a bit of back-story about your business or your product, to put the main story in context. But at all costs avoid the temptation to pack everything into the press release. You'll just confuse and overwhelm and alienate the journalist. Instead add a section after the press release called 'note to editors' or 'background information' or something like that. That's where you can explain that you've been in business X months and you supply Y widgets to Z countries.

You won't have to spend long looking at newspapers or magazines to see how the pictures they use tend to be radically different from the snapshots that most of us take in our private and family lives.

Good press pictures are good in two ways: both equally important. First, they are technically good in terms of being well composed, lit and shot. They'll be in focus. They won't have red-eye from flash. They won't have lamp-posts growing out of the subject's head. And so on. That much is obvious really. Never send photographs out with press releases that look in any way like home snapshots. To put it bluntly , the journalist will not only not use the photograph, but will be less likely to use the story at all. Bad pictures can kill a good story. They're that important.

A good picture also means a picture that adds to the story and helps to tell the story or to underline some part of it. A good press release picture is one that is engaging and impactful in its own right. I can't explain in detail what that picture might look like, but it is likely to feature one or more of the following elements:

- people smiling genuinely (at each other as well as at the camera);

- dramatic contrast of some kind (of height, age, size, strength);

- action and motion (as long as it's all in focus);

- large numbers of people;

- unusual angles of view (looking up, or down, at something);

- emotion;

- humour.

There are many things to avoid, but in business PR the absolute no-no is the shaking hands shot. Avoid at all costs.

If in doubt always hire a photographer. But always hire one who has done a lot of PR. They're easy to find and the good ones are very good. Don't use a wedding photographer. With no disrespect, it's a completely different skill.

It almost goes without saying, but anyway, make sure your press release, not just your covering note, has all your contact details (phone and email are most important, and nobody's going to fax you so don't worry about that).

Arguably even more important than the construction of your press release and the creation of your photographs is the selection of your media list (the list of people you're going to send your release to). The simple rule of thumb is relevance. If your story concerns sports in some way then it's legitimate to send it to sports editors. Otherwise don't. If you send out blanket emails to everyone at the local paper you could get branded a spammer and they won't like you. And if they don't like you they won't use your press releases. That's why they call it media 'relations' after all.

So make a list of the kind of journalists you want to communicate with (business, general news, cookery, television, travel). Let's say you're launching a new holiday business of some kind. You'll want to approach business journalists and travel/holiday journalists. There's no point at all in approaching cookery editors **unless** your holiday business is focused on cooking experiences, in which case they become relevant. It's all about relevance.

The next task is to make a list of media: national media, regional and local media, specialist media. As you make your list (and don't forget radio and TV), consider this question: can I 'really' picture my story in here? If you're not sure take a closer look at the kind of story they do run. Look for the little mentions of stories a bit like yours. So now you've got a list of media and list of kinds of journalists. Now you need to make contact. Don't be scared.

It's a simple process: find the paper or magazine's website and look for the main contact number. Call them and and explain very simply that you wish to speak to the (select type of) editor about a news release. Don't try to explain the story to the switchboard person.

Two things might happen. They will put you through or they will give you a general email address to use. Either is fine but the first is better. If you get through to a real live journalist, first check they are the relevant journalist (obviously). Then explain simply and confidently that you are carrying out a PR exercise for (your company name) and that you would like to send them a press release about your new widget. That's all and enough.

Most journalists will say "sure, send it to me". Then make sure you get their email and (ideally) a phone number. Keep it short and professional: don't tell them the story, just that you think they might be interested and that you appreciate them taking the time to look at it. Then you send them the 'package' as we've discussed already. A day or so later, I recommend that you call them (which is why it's helpful to get their number) to follow up. This is really just a courtesy call but it can be a help. Journalists are busy and your call can help to prompt them gently to look at the story in case they haven't got round to it.

The process of this kind of PR is not difficult: but you absolutely need to allow yourself the time and the space to do it well. It will pay you huge dividends.

Brand Builder Workout

Today's workout is not complex, but it is challenging. Using the guidelines in this chapter try to write a press release announcing some (real) news about your brand. Read it and re-read it. Now, the ultimate test: contact a journalist on your local paper (or your industry-specific trade magazine) and ask if you can send them your press release. Tell them that it's your first time and you're trying to get it right. Ask them if they would look at it and let you know if it gives them what they need.

THE EXPERT VIEW

Gordon Maw, Maw Communications

Why should my business engage with the media?

PR deals with two key things: reputation and awareness. It can help provide independent endorsement for your organization or your individuals; it can enhance your reputation and increase awareness of what you do. For many companies, PR can help to create an environment where other advertising works harder – so if people have heard of you and they respect you, they are more likely to respond to your other messages.

While PR is a broad church these days, the elements that are dependent on journalist-based content are principally concerned with the medium of 'news'. Therefore, any attempt to work with this media must be based within the context of news. 'News' means something people haven't heard already. You have to put yourself in the journalist's shoes and remember that a journalist is part private investigator, part screenwriter. If you want to work with journalists effectively, you've got to be able to appeal to both parts – give them something that is new and relevant to their readers and help them to paint pictures and make the story come to life.

Ten tips for working with the press effectively:

1. Find your news in actual events: new staff, company results, a new promotional campaign, a major expansion, a new

office, winning an award, an accreditation, a new team, a new department, a new logo/brand, a new website, a new office, an event, a new bit of kit, a new product launch, a new deal, a new contract, a big new client, an internal team building event, staff having triplets, staff that excel outside of work...

2. Get to know your media – find out which media is relevant to you, look at the kind of stories they cover and how they do them and then start building a relationship with them. PR is based on relationships; on the premise that it is very hard to do business with people you don't know. Think about how you could meet the journalists either by suggesting a meeting over coffee or a lunch or by approaching them at networking events.

3. If you really want to get your message across, pick up the phone and engage the journalist directly. Be prepared, be confident, make your story different. In short, help the journalist understand why he should cover your story.

4. Learn how to write great press releases. That means great headers, pithy quotes and being able to convey the context of the story in the first couple of paragraphs.

5. Insight and research – you won't always have a 'hard news' peg or a 'world exclusive', so sometimes you need to generate 'news out of nothing'. One of the most common tools is research. This can be consumer or market research commissioned through a specialist research agency or it could be based on your own desk research of a particular issue.

6. Don't be afraid to use the traditional PR Holy Trinity: charity, sponsorship, awards. –They have conveyed strong messages about organizations for years and still work today.

7. Become an industry expert – there is a strong possibility that you know more about your industry and the issues that impact it than anyone else in your area. That insight is precious and very valuable to journalists. You need to learn how to put it into context and how to use it in a way that benefits yourself and the media.

8. Talk about the big things and people will think you're big – Virgin Atlantic had one plane when they launched but they chose to go head to head with British Airways who had over 300. Customers and the industry believed that they were a genuine rival to BA rather than an upstart with one plane!

9. Give your news a twist – news is better when completely unexpected. For example: an energy provider telling people to turn their heating on during an August heatwave to test the pipes.

10. PR is a visual art – most newspapers contain more photographs than articles so invest in photography. A professional photographer could charge £100–£150 for a session, but it could cost you more in wasted time to do your story without a picture.

You can't ignore the revolution taking place in online PR. Within a lifetime's memory, people queued in the street to buy a copy of the *Daily Express* because it was the best way to find out what was going on. Today, many people are just as likely to hear about something for the first time via Facebook or twitter. But how can you harness the web for PR purposes?

- Researching journalists: the web offers a range of tools for researching journalists and the things they write about. In addition to simply Googling, there are free tools such as www. journalisted.com, a not-for-profit website built to make it easier for the public to find out more about journalists and what they write about.

- Press release distribution: there is a proliferation of online press release distribution sites that can complement your traditional distribution as well as your SEO activity. They offer services designed to send your release direct to media websites in a number of different ways.

- Online research tools: there was a time when commissioning some research meant paying a fortune for a traditional research agency. Now there are a range of options, from creating your own surveys online that you can send to your own database, right up to online omnibus surveys that allow you to survey a sample of the UK population.

- Online journalist networking: a lot of journalists are active bloggers and Twitter users and it is an increasingly common way to build relationships. Many journalists will talk about the articles they are trying to write or ask for help on Twitter.

- Blogging: the reality these days is that a blog posting about your organization can be just as likely to appear on page one of a Google search as an article about you in the *FT*. As a result, you have to take blogs seriously and work out how your organization deals with them.

- Monitoring press coverage: you may not have your own press cuttings service to monitor your brand and your coverage but there are an array of powerful free tools online. Google Alert, for example, can search the internet for any relevant terms in news or blogs.

- Google: the first step for many people when checking out a company is to Google them – so your Google footprint (the first couple of pages of search results) has a huge say on your reputation. But you can influence it. Newspaper websites, blogs, online press release distribution sites, networking sites like LinkedIn and more traditional business networks such as the Chamber of Commerce all have highly optimized websites. That means that working with the right sites can ensure that your good news and key messages will appear high up in any search engine results page.

Gordon Maw is the former Director of Communications of Virgin Money and founder of specialist PR agency MAW Communications which provides both consumer and business-to-business PR solutions. You can find out more at www.mawcomms.co.uk

REAL BRAND STORY

Jess Morgan

Singer-songwriter Jess Morgan explains how she has made herself and her music stand out from the crowd by maintaining independent artistic and 'brand' control.

I've been writing my own songs and wanting to do it for a living for about 3–4 years now. It took me the first year to realize the way things are in the music industry now and to really embrace fighting the good fight all by myself. It's become my aim to take my music as far as possible by myself. I think in life it's your experiences – good and bad – that shape you. In music it's the same. I hope to one day stand out as a musician because I have chased the experiences, travelled, met exciting people, met horrible people, been disappointed, exhausted, invigorated and worked hard. I suppose I am building my own stories and developing myself as the storyteller. My own experiences, though often unrelated to the songs, are making this happen.

My self-released e.p. in summer 2009 was the biggest challenge I've come up against so far. After talks after talks about deals, recordings, money stuff, it became fairly clear that there wasn't much at this point that a record label could do for me that I couldn't just do for myself: thus the name I decided upon for my own record label *Amateur Boxer Records*. It was very much a case of feeling my way through the dark at first, but I found most people in the know were fairly willing to share their knowledge in exchange for a bit of tea and a cake!

Constant gigging is helping me to gain experience and to build a reputation. Live performances, I feel, are the best way for me to showcase what it is I do. That way, each performance is individual, so naturally with subtle changes in the delivery, the story told is a little differently each time. I like it that way.

I'll travel as far as I need to go to get to a gig – which is often unpaid(!) – but I find the on-the-road lifestyle inspiring and motivating. Ideas of travelling troubadours and our nomadic ancestry fill me with enormous sense of purpose and allow me to give my performances the energy to hopefully make an impression.

I suppose the way I think about music is really very idealistic. A huge part of the image I seem to put across is something that is unintentional – not something I devised or designed: that I am hugely passionate about my genre of music and I do see music as an art form. People do not expect me to be a business woman alongside this and the extent of my ambitions have been underestimated. To be honest, a big part of releasing my own e.p. was to show myself and a lot of other people what I can do – and that I'm not just sitting around *waiting* for things to happen.

I suppose another thing that is perhaps in conflict with the business side of Jess Morgan is the personal touch I like to give things, like the demos I send out, my CDs and my website. For example, I'll always hand-write a letter or note to go with any CD I send out – whether that's to a DJ, a Radio Plugger or someone buying my CD mail-order from my website. Obviously with the mail order CDs I am mostly thanking that person for taking several minutes out of their day to think about my music. It's only polite to say thanks. Where mail is often unsolicited such as to the DJs, the pluggers, the events managers, etc., I try to give that person an extra reason to play my record. The first time I sent a demo to Steve Lamacq in 2007 he mentioned the hand-written letter I had written with it – and has subsequently played everything I have sent him since then. Sure – he's a notorious and well re-spected DJ – but he's also a nice guy who just appreciates a bit of politeness!

My website has taken on many forms. However, I find that by building my page out of a free weblogging service I have the ad-vantage of being able to update my site from anywhere in the world. I can even text my website these days! I travel a lot now – and as I've explained, the travel is a strong part of who I am, and something people seem to enjoy reading about as it's happening. By combining elements of myspace and youtube in my website, I can blog, show a gig calendar and let people know all about me really, with the minimum of hassle and the freedom to do it on the road.

To create my logo I simply typed out Jess Morgan in the standard type-face Georgia. I printed this and then drew over it in marker pen and scanned it back into the computer. This way I end up with a traditional, no-frills font but with the look of being hand-drawn. At the moment my website is themed with some of the same design features of the e.p.

I have a linocut print ready to form the artwork for the full-length album which is very simple but bold. I expect to change the theme colours of the website to match this. It's taken me a couple of years to decide on a way to present all my stuff and I'm finally able to say that things are cohesive and that hopefully if someone were to have me confused with another Jess Morgan (there are a few of us), they'd be able to find the things associated with me by the design and the approach.

Day 21

How Not to Waste Your Advertising Budget

Most (but not all) advertising by small businesses is simply wasted money. But why does most advertising fail? Here are just a few reasons:

- Lack of clarity about what the advertising is meant to achieve (brand awareness, sales generation and brand positioning are just some of the possibilities).

- Advertising to the wrong people, in the wrong place, at the wrong time.

- Lack of understanding about advertising's potential and its limitations.

- Lack of somebody really skillful to conceive, write, art-direct (design) the ad.

- Trying to do much too much with one advertisement.

- Not having enough budget to allow your ads to appear enough times and with sufficient frequency.

- Thinking that advertising is just about grabbing attention.

- Thinking that advertising is just about communicating facts.

- Thinking that advertising is about making rational, persuasive arguments about your product or service.

Still, there's nothing wrong with advertising, if you use it properly. In fact, in the right circumstances you can't beat it, and at some point you're probably going to want and need to use its unique strengths. So when does advertising have merit?

- When you're clear about what you're trying to achieve with it.

- When you are advertising to the right people, at the right time, in the right place.

- When you understand what advertising can and can't do.

- When you hire (or persuade) someone very skillful to write your ad and someone equally skillful to design it.

- When your ad just tries to do just one thing. One thing. One.

- When you've got enough money to run your ad enough times, in enough places, with enough frequency, over a long enough period for people to notice it, notice it again, notice it again…

- When you know it's not enough to shout at people to grab attention.

- When you know that it's not enough to tell people facts.

- When you know that advertising **never** works by making rational argument (no matter how persuasively written).

If you're thinking about advertising for your business, please work your way through the questions and tasks in this chapter before you spend any money. So many small businesses in particular get their fingers burned and their money wasted by diving straight in to advertising.

If I'm sounding cautious about advertising, it's from the position of experience. I was a board director of two advertising agencies, as well as a copywriter (the bloke who dreams up ad concepts and then writes them) and a Creative Director (leading a team of very skilled people creating ads of every kind, for radio and TV as well as press). We made some great advertising that worked for our clients. I think we made plenty of advertising that didn't have any benefit to anyone at all (certainly not our clients) except perhaps to the owners of the newspapers and the TV stations where we advertised. It wasn't because we weren't very clever. It was because we were naturally predisposed to recommend advertising as the best solution when actually something quite different might have been more appropriate and more effective in achieving the marketing aims of the client.

Look at the following list of possible objectives for creating an advertising campaign. Put a tick next to any which match what you want to achieve with your campaign.

- I want more people to know that my brand exists.

- I want people to understand what my brand means.

- I want people to be aware of my particular product or service.

- I want people to phone the number on the ad to buy my product or service.

- I want people to visit my website to buy my products or service.

- I want people to visit my shop/café/restaurant.

Did you tick more than one? Go back and look again. If you've ticked more than one then your advertising will fail. Or at the very least it will be compromized and less effective than you hope. Whatever you do in advertising, do it simply and single-mindedly.

Brand Builder Workout

To test the single message theory try the following exercise. Spend half an hour with any Sunday newspaper. Within the main paper and all the various sections, supplements and magazines, you will find advertising of pretty much every kind.

You'll find car ads in the colour magazine (most telling you about a new product, but others really focused on reminding you what the particular brand stands for). In the culture section you'll find ads for entertainers and bands on tour. These are, in effect, product or service ads. They're letting you know something is happening. They don't try to explain who the band is. It's assumed that you know that by other means. And if you don't know, then you can assume the ad isn't aimed at you.

In the same section you'll find ads for stage shows or movies. Now you'll see that these ones frequently contain short snippets from reviews. They don't explain what the show is about but they are assuring you that it's worth going to see. The reviews are doing the brand job for these ads.

Now look at the financial pages and check out the ads for the investment companies. Think about what they're doing. Alerting you to a new product with a competitive interest rate perhaps. Or reminding you of their bona fides with a few performance ratings from recent years or perhaps with a review from a commentator (much like the theatre productions). But take note that they are rarely, if ever, trying to do more than one job with any one ad.

Finally, look at the small ads in the back of the weekend or leisure sections. This is where you will find the ads from the rocking horse makers, for the children's clothes catalogues, for the back-saving gardening implements, and the luxury bedding and so on. Go through these ads in particular and do some analysis. Which ones are obeying the rule of clarity and simplicity? Which ones try to cram in too much information? Which ones are about raising awareness, or about increasing your understanding and appreciation of the brand, and which are about wanting you to take action right now (to phone or visit a website to buy or to request a catalogue)?

The golden rule is to know the one thing you're trying to achieve. One thing.

A key to success in advertising is to be absolutely clear about your audience. This list should help. Which of the following are your targets?

- People in the neighbourhood who might want to visit my shop/café/garage, etc.

- People widely geographically scattered who have some particular interest in common and to whom my product or service is relevant.

- People who at any time, in any place, might be looking for a solution to a particular problem for which my product/service is relevant.

- People looking for new ideas and trends.

- People whose main interest is getting value for money.

Brand Builder Workout

The list below isn't exhaustive. In fact it's just the beginning of an exercise. Try to write down a description of your intended audience as follows:

- What kind of people are they?

- How old are they likely to be?

- Where do they live (locally, across the country, all over the world)?

- What are they interested in?

- What do they need?

- What do they want (it's not the same as need. I might need a collar for my cat, but I might want one that's studded with diamonds)?

- Is price important to them?

There isn't room in this book to address this audience profiling in detail, but you should be able to come up with a reasonably accurate outline description of the people for whom you are creating your advertising. The more clearly you can describe your target audience the more likely you are to be able to find them, or rather to put your advertising in places where they will find it. And even more importantly, you will be infinitely more likely to create advertising which will engage them and stand some chance of being effective in getting your (single) message across.

The next stage in creating effective advertising is to decide where to advertise. The quickest route to success is to try to choose media that matches your audience as you've described them. If your audience is strictly limited to a small locality, for example, say one neighbourhood of your town, then it makes sense to think locally and to use a local newsletter or magazine. But if your audience is defined by interest or attitude rather than locality, and you can genuinely serve a widely scattered audience then maybe a special interest magazine (or website perhaps) is right for you.

And so on. It's not a difficult process provided that you stay focused and disciplined, always trying to match your audience to possible places to advertise.

Pay per click advertising needs a special mention here. It's a whole subject area of its own, but as a form of advertising it can be highly effective for small business. The great advantage of PPC advertising (the biggest provider being Google Adwords) is that people only find your ad when they are specifically searching for the kind of thing that you provide. To achieve effective PPC advertising of course needs some skill; you need to write your ad carefully and choose your keywords (the search terms that people will be looking for) even more carefully. But Google itself provides lots of advice, and there's heaps more advice about PPC all over the web.

A final few words on advertising. Resist all approaches by newspapers or any other media offering you special deals, special features or anything else that you haven't planned in advance. An advertising agency can be very useful here in working out a detailed advertising schedule for you. Whether you do it, or an agency does it for you, make a schedule of your intended advertising (and budget) and stick to it. No matter how friendly or charming the sales person offering the special deal. No matter how tempting the great value offer, say "No". If it's not on your planned schedule of advertising spend, then don't do it. Remember, media sales people are not interested in your advertising effectiveness, only in selling the space.

THE EXPERT VIEW

Chris Murphy, Chairman, balloon dog

Advertising from the agency point of view

Advertising – it's all around us, sometimes we love it, sometimes it irritates us but it has become a part of our culture. It can entertain but it is at its most powerful when it engages and informs customers and moves them closer to purchasing your product or service.

The very word 'advertising' has evolved to encompass many forms of communication, from the sign on a shop to a TV campaign. It is a generic term in much the same way as 'biro' can be used to describe different types of writing implements. But here I want to look at traditional forms of advertising that require the advertiser (the company promoting itself) to pay for the media that it uses – space in a paper or magazine, a commercial on TV, airtime on radio, a poster site and the like. Advertising agencies can give expert advice on which medium is best suited to your needs and business goals and also on what the creative idea to convey your message could be. So the notes that follow are intended to be a guide for businesses to manage their brand advertising themselves or for briefing an agency.

The start point for any advertising is to know what you want it to achieve. Often it is the beginning of a relationship not an end in itself, so be clear in the objective. It may simply be awareness of your brand, it may be a specific event or promotion or it could be to direct people to another source of more information (website, order a catalogue, visit a shop, etc.). Whenever possible, have a single message in advertising – it is easier for your customer to take in and allows more creative opportunity. Some of the most iconic advertising has expressed just one message – 'the future's bright, the future's Orange' was just about establishing the brand name; 'compare the meerkat' is about getting people to the Compare the Market website.

Then you need to understand your customers enough to know which media they read or watch – accurate targeting will reduce wastage and increase your effectiveness. Media owners have details of who their audience are and you can overlay this with the type of people you sell to. And the same media can talk to different people; think of the different sections in the *Sunday Times* – between them they talk to a wide range of people. As well as who they are, the more you know what they think and want the better. Never be afraid to ask them whether by using commissioned research, creating an online questionnaire on your website or simply talking to customers you meet – the more you know the more relevant your advertising is and the more effective it is.

Furthermore, as your knowledge grows so the relevance of direct mail grows. It is easy to think of it as 'junk mail', as sadly that is what a lot of it is, but if you give the right message to the right people in the right way then the returns can be significant and directly measurable – you know who you mailed and if they responded. This form of advertising is often questioned because too many brands use it as 'mass mail' as opposed to direct or personalized mail.

When it comes to creativity in your advertising – the **really** fun bit – the need for clarity of message has already been mentioned but two other factors can make the difference between success and failure. First, don't overlook the basics of 'who , what, where' – ensure all advertising includes who the brand is, the message you want to convey (remember ideally it's just the one message!) and where the customer can find out more.

Second, as you plan what you want your advertising to achieve put in place mechanisms to track the results. A micro site for example (a website specifically linked to the ad that is part of your main website, which you can track visitors to), dedicated telephone numbers or redeemable vouchers are three such methods.

And finally, always remember that your advertising is part of a journey that customers will go on with your brand and as such is just one element that will shape their view of the brand and ultimately whether to buy it or not. There is no better example of this than Virgin Atlantic. We had a family holiday to New York: I saw an ad that promised special deals, went online and there they were clearly shown on the home page. Booking was easy, the in-flight experience very good and all consistently delivered with ease and friendliness. But then came the really powerful moment. I wrote to customer services on our return and thanked them for the excellent service and named the cabin crew who had looked after us so well. The response I got was not an automated 'we appreciate all feedback and note your comments' but a personalized message referring to the details of my note and even told me how long the stewardess had been with them!

The tone of the very first advert I saw and the promise of an engaging customer experience was delivered from beginning to end. Always make sure you can deliver the promise your advertising conveys.

Always an 'ad agency man', Chris Murphy created his first agency through an MBO in 1990, forming Fox Murphy seven years later, and rebranding as balloon dog in 2008. The agency employs some 65 people in Norwich and London and works with clients including Barclays and Pret A Manger. See www.balloondog.co.uk

Day 22

MAKING YOUR BRAND COME ALIVE ONLINE

If you are under the age of, say, 40 then I don't, frankly, have much to tell you about the web itself that you don't already know. Actually it has so quickly become such a huge part of our lives that even that age demarcation seems a bit random, and very conservative. Suffice to say that we are absolutely, incontrovertibly, utterly woven into the web. We buy holidays and travel online. We bank online. We order groceries, books, CDs, DVDs and games online. Increasingly we download or stream our entertainment, from TV shows that we've missed to music, to movies.

Enough said, I think. I don't need to explain the web any more than I need to explain newspapers. Besides, if you are interested in the phenomenon of the web itself, its development and potential, then by far the best place to look is, well, on the web! Dive in.

What you do need to consider, though, is how to bring your brand alive on the web, because bring it alive there you must. There aren't many absolute mandatory must-dos in this book, but here is one. If you want to create a brand that is worthy of the name, then it **must** have an engaging and compelling web life.

Five years ago I might not have been so adamant about this. Now, however, it is beyond all doubt. This is the year in which you must take your brand online, imaginatively, actively, conversationally, even argumentatively. So this short chapter avoids technical issues of the web and instead lays out some simple principles and gives you some specific tasks which will all add up to enhancing your brand exponentially through its online life. And one of the beautiful and satisfying things about this is that it barely costs any money at all (although it does cost time and effort).

There are four strands of activity that a brand needs to address on the web. Different activities are required for each and different results can be achieved. You don't have to do them all at once, but the more you do then the more your brand will come alive, potentially right around the globe.

First and most obviously is your brand's website, your basic toehold in the online world. Of course, almost everyone and his auntie has a website already, and my guess is that if you already have a business then you already have a website too. If that's the case and you've already got one, then I want you to go to it now and to look at it seriously, trying as hard as possible to look at it through the eyes of an outsider, someone coming to your site for the first time. While you do that, I want you to ask yourself these questions and to answer them honestly. No, **really** honestly.

- Is this website classy? Is it visually attractive and engaging? Is it nice to be there?

- Is it clear and easy to find your way about your website? Is it obvious where to click to go to the pages you want to go to (remember you're imagining you've arrived here for the first time)?

- Does it offer information that is useful and interesting?

- If it's a site for buying things from (e-commerce), is it really easy to do the buying bit?

- If someone makes a mistake or gets lost, is it easy to retrace their steps, or do they have to start all over again (because they won't, you know... they'll go somewhere else)?

- Are there any reasons for people to come back to your website apart from the purely transactional ones of wanting to buy stuff (i.e. opportunities to win stuff or get free stuff, or a regularly updated blog, or a discussion forum, or customer feedback and reviews)?

- Finally, how does your website compare to your competitors? Does it make you proud or a bit embarrassed?

If the answer to any of these questions is anything less than glowingly self-confident, in other words if you aren't genuinely convinced that your site is as good as it can be, then you need to pay attention to this before you look at any other aspect of your online activity. After all, your website is your place on the web, your brand's home turf.

Before we move on from the site itself, take a look at the sites of a few brands mentioned in this book: Byfords, First Direct, Adnams, Mr. Site, Further, Special Design Studio are just a few examples. Every one of them has been thought through from top to bottom and constructed and designed by professionals who have kept the 'brand' very high in their priorities throughout the process.

But before you protest that this is all very well if you've got plenty of money, let me make an important point: there are fundamentally two good ways of creating a website. And one of them costs very little.

The first (not the cheap one) is to hire a specialist web company, or a graphic design practice working closely with a web development firm, to design and create your website for you. Frankly, for any brand other than a tiny 'lifestyle' business, this is the route I would recommend. Buying the services of specialists like this is not without its difficulties (even more challenging than hiring a designer for your visual identity) but I would strongly recommend talking to at least three firms, and only consider those from whom you can get client recommendations (from clients you can actually talk to).

It's impossible for me to put even a ball park figure on what a professional website might cost you. The variables are too many and too great. Just make sure of two things:

- that the company you choose gives you a detailed, fixed quotation covering all the costs of the project (including ongoing costs like hosting);

- that the designer understands your brand thoroughly.

Finally, and I mention this only because every conversation I have ever had with 'web-people' has featured this phrase, be clear about whether you want (and whether you really need) a content-managed site. A content-managed site is one which is constructed to allow you (that is you personally or one of your team) to alter the content via a kind of digital back door.

With some content-managed sites the owner (you) has access to everything on the site, but more usually your access will be restricted to, say, the blog or news pages, or to particular areas where you might need to change product information.

Now in my experience web developers really don't like content-managed sites, for two reasons. First, because they are a bit more complex to create, and second (and more importantly) because every time you go in through the back door to 'tweak' your site there is a risk that you'll do something inadvertently which will screw the site up completely. I know this because I've done it and I've heard numerous stories of site owners (usually people like me who know nothing about web programming) accidentally destroying, or temporarily compromising, their own sites. Actually there is an even more subtle danger, which is that whilst you might not break anything, you might well just move enough things around (a bit of text here, a picture there) that you can easily spoil the visual integrity of the site. And you can't blame the designer or the developer when you've done so. It's your fault. And the reason that web developers don't like this is because the first thing we bulls in the china shop do when we've started to break things is to phone them up crying, "my site doesn't work, please can you fix it."

So if you really need some access to amend information on your site (but only if you really, really need this) then talk to your web developer about a content-managed site. But be prepared to pay more for the privilege and to have a service agreement with them for when you mess your site up and call them in a panic. Otherwise steer clear of content management and agree a simple charging structure with your developer for when you ask them to change things. Much safer, frankly. After all, you've got a brand to look after, should you really be fiddling around on your website?

Despite my strong preference for professionally designed and built websites I have to acknowledge here that there is another really affordable way into the world of the web, using one form or another of DIY website package. Some of these are very easy to use (if you go slowly and carefully), others less so. Some are free (with the proviso that you have to allow banner advertising to run on your site, over which you have no control). There are usually upgrade packages available for a fee, which allow you to get rid of the ads.

The various providers (you can search for them easily with any search engine) offer different packages including the option of site hosting, registration of your website name, etc. I'll leave you to explore the possibilities. Suffice to say that they can work very well if your business is fairly simple and straightforward, and if you don't mind choosing from a range of design templates for your site. You can alter colours and images and so on but you will never get the freedom in design terms that you can achieve with a professionally designed site.

If budget is tight then do consider this route, but please bear in mind the importance of your website. It's your brand's presence on the web. I have used, or at least tried out, several providers, including Weebly, Webs, and Mr. Site (whose own brand story is featured in this book). All of them will work well if you have the time, and the 'eye', to use them skilfully (much like any other DIY activity some folk will do it brilliantly, others um... not so brilliantly).

Your next step after (and only after) you've established a website that you're really proud of, is to explore other online environments to which you can take your brand, to showcase it or tell people about your goods and services.

Obvious examples include Ebay and other online market places, aggregate sites such as those offering insurance and other financial services products, travel market places such as lastminute.com and many others. You can negotiate to be featured in the listings on these sites, or you can simply buy advertising space on them.

A few hours on the web will reveal a wide range of potential outlets that are relevant to your particular sector, and which may or may not suit your specific business and brand.

A word of caution, though. In one way or another (either by direct fee or commission), you will almost certainly have to pay for the privilege of taking part in someone else's market place. Take that into account whilst deciding whether this is the right route for you.

And remember, what we are trying to do is build a 'brand' for the long term, not just flog some stuff in the short term. So if the online market places that are available to you help you to enhance your brand and bring it to a wider audience, then that's a good thing. If, on the other hand, they look like they might undermine or compromise your brand, then be very cautious. Note how a couple of very high profile insurance companies make a big issue in their advertising about not being available on aggregate sites. They are protecting their brand from what I often refer to as 'commodity hell'.

The three biggest areas of opportunity for small brands on the web are 'search' (making your website easy to find), 'social media' (Facebook, twitter and the rest) and 'TV on Web' (the latest big thing). All three can be important to your brand, but all three are big and complex topics in their own right. This book can only touch the surface, and to do that I've asked an expert in each area, Mark Cook, Stephanie Diamond and Fiona Ryder to give you an introduction, and they follow this chapter, back to back.

I think you'll find their advice exciting and inspiring.

THE EXPERT VIEW

The five most important things you can do to optimize your site for search engines

Mark Cook, Search Marketing Director, Further Search Marketing

1. ***Don't mak e things worse for the user:*** Changes should never be made to your website or content in the name of search engine optimization that have a negative impact on the user. This includes things such as the popular but false myth that keyword stuffing (repeating the same keyword over and over within text) will significantly help you with search engine positioning. Search engines are generally looking for things that improve user experience, so if anything your website should be easier to use and friendlier to users after it has been optimized for search engines.

   Get some help from Google The 'rules' of search engine optimization can change along with what is considered best practice. While Google won't give you the inside track on how to rank well in their search engine, they do give you a push in the right direction, highlighting what you should and should not be doing in both their SEO Guidelines and Webmaster Guidelines.

   Make page titles clear It seems simple, but the humble page title is still one of the most important on-page metrics for search engines to judge the content of your page. Best practice is keeping your title concise, with the key phrase (not a list of keywords) that you're targeting at the start. This title is also the first thing the user will see in a search results page, so once again, you're helping users see what your page is about and improving your chances of ranking well.

Use internal links wisely   One of the most common mistakes we find as an agency is with a website's internal links. Google uses the anchor text (the text present in a link) to determine the content of the following page. This means, it increases your chances of ranking by linking to internal pages with keywords. So, a good example would be 'We have a special offer on **red widgets**', with 'red widgets' as the link. A bad example would be '**Click here** to see our red widgets special offer'. Relevant hyperlinks also help the user, as typically people 'scan read' web pages and their eye is drawn to navigational links. Having descriptive anchor text will help them more quickly locate the page they need to get to.

Create outstanding content   The foundation of ranking well in any of the major search engines comes down to one thing: links. This means getting other relevant and popular websites to link to you. The concept is very easy to understand. The more websites that link to a specific page, the more indication there is to search engines that this is a very useful page, so it should rank higher. Unfortunately, the process of getting links is not an easy one, with some people breaking Google's guidelines and buying links and spammers bombarding forums with them. There is one solid, proven and reliable technique that will get you links and it won't change. Create outstanding content. We don't mean, 'informative', 'good', 'mediocre' content, but invest some of your marketing budget to improving the information you offer. If you provide real value, whether it's original research, inside information or a collation of the lot, it needs to be special. When people find value, they will naturally share this with their peers which means links from blogs, forums and social networks. With more content becoming user-generated and the increasing reliance on social media to find quality content, the benefit of providing value is only likely to increase in the future. Your reward for your effort is high search engine rankings.

Mark Cook is Search Marketing Director at award-winning Further Search Marketing, one of the UK's fastest-growing search and social media marketing agencies. To find out more, visit www.further.co.uk

THE EXPERT VIEW

Getting started in social media marketing

Stephanie Diamond, President, Digital Media Works, Inc.

There are a multitude of ways to use the social media tools to connect with your perfect audience depending on your personality and your business goals. There are, however, some concepts and strategies you can use to make your entry into this type of marketing easier and more successful.

Let's start with some concepts.

Establishing a dialogue

Conversation is the most effective way to spread your message and gain attention online. The value to you is that you find people who are searching for your solutions and are ready to make a buying decision.

Readers should trust you and turn to you for suggestions about your topic of expertise. Assure your customer that you can understand and provide solutions to their problems and this message will be carried to others who can benefit from it. Networking online gives you opportunity to connect with like-minded partners around the world who you would never have had the opportunity to meet in person.

Providing a high perceived value

Add value to every part of your customer interaction so that you stand above other brands as the clear choice.

So what are the assets that every business owner has that they can draw on to show value?

- Life experience that gives everything you say and do a valuable context – knowing when to apply what advice

- Relationships with online influencers and other colleagues

- Networks of which you are a part – online communities, forum participation, social networks

- Testimonials and case studies from satisfied customers

- Your current products and services

- Raw materials of all kinds – audios, articles, etc.

- Your active lists of customers and prospects

Communication of personal influence

On the web you have the opportunity to speak one-to-one on a mass scale. However, if you don't help your customer see the value you provide, you are wasting your time. Your message will not be heard or spread.

Niche targeting of customers

Describing and targeting your niche audience is central to being successful online. You don't want to take a scattershot approach and hope you'll be found. A study of who your customers are, where they go to get their information and what problems they want to solve will go a long way to helping your business accelerate its growth.

What are the tools and tactics of SMM?

A social media tool is one that allows your customer to make their opinions known to you and others. Some examples are:

- A Facebook fan page – people join your 'club' to show support and interest in you

- Twitter – an online social network that allows you to communicate a message to all your 'followers' in 140 characters. This also allows you to point people who are interested in hearing your message to anywhere on the web you want to take them

- Customer reviews – people can tell you and other customers what they think of your product and services

- Blogs – you share your thoughts and information with people who can comment and share their opinions with you

- Forums – groups of like-minded people meet online to share information and answer questions for one another

- Suggestion boxes online – customers can tell you how you can improve products and services

How does all this translate into content for your social media marketing efforts?

Here are some things to remember when you are creating your online content from social media marketing:

Provide your information in a variety of formats: audios, videos, PDFs and checklists will supply your customers with a format of their choice.

Have information for each of your customer's buying stages handy. Make sure both the person who is starting their search and the one who is ready to buy have the information they need to make a buying decision.

Make sure to include the keywords your customers will use to find you. Know what words people are using to find you and weave them into all your information.

Stephanie Diamond, founder of Digital Media Works, Inc., is a 20+ year marketing professional with experience building profits in over 75 different industries. Stephanie helps small business owners discover profitable assets hidden in their businesses. You can read her blog at www. marketingmessageblog.com

THE EXPERT VIEW

How to use TV and video on the web as a powerful brand building tool.

Fiona Ryder, Chief Executive Officer, StreamExchange

Start with the message. Whether you intend to create one video, many videos or an entire web TV channel, think about what you want to say, how you want to say it and your intended audience.

Consider the purpose of the message. Since video on the web is such a versatile tool, you need to ask yourself what its purpose is. Do you want to educate, entertain, create a call to action for people to buy your products or contact you – or a combination of some or all of the above?

You then need to think about the life span of the 'campaign'. Is it just a single video release or is this a longer-term initiative that will need to be updated? Many companies just want to improve their brand and corporate position by demonstrating that they are an authority on a particular subject. Others want to build an audience that may return to a web TV channel frequently and thus build brand loyalty in the process.

Think of a supermarket chain that wants to create an online cooking channel using products and ingredients which it sells in its stores. This would have the benefit of educating an audience, providing something useful and offering viewers the opportunity to buy any product they might be missing in order to create a recipe demonstrated on the channel. Thus this is both useful to the consumer and to the supermarket. The additional net benefit is that it should create a positive brand effect for the supermarket in the process reaffirming its position and brand story.

Next you need to consider where your intended audience will find your video or video channel. On your site, on a partner or an affiliate site, on a publisher's site – or just on a video aggregation or sharing site like YouTube or Daily Motion? If you are a plumbing supply shop, perhaps you might want to show customers how to mend a leaking tap using products from your online or real world shop. You can host the finished video on your own site – perhaps creating your own DIY web TV channel in the process, or upload it to Video Jug or 5min – sites which host 'How To' videos.

The way the video is shot is an essential part of the branding process and must reflect your business. For instance, if you run a small boutique hotel you could show potential customers your environment; but the way that the video is shot is as important as the content itself. High quality, slow motion images of feather beds being made, champagne being poured and exquisitely presented food being served is a very different video to a quick video tour of a couple of rooms in the hotel and an interview with the owner.

Finally, think about your own visual branding and the way that the video will appear to customers – both on your site and on others. If the video is to be displayed on your site do you really want to use another company's branding on the video player? YouTube, Daily Motion and others have wonderful tools to enable you to upload your video to their site and then embed that video simply by pasting a line of code into your web page; but a word of caution here. Whilst third party video players are easy to use, you really should consider what message this might convey about your business or company. Hotmail email addresses work perfectly well. but don't always give out the right impression about a company or business. Similarly a YouTube player on a company's own website makes a branding statement and, I would argue, not always a good one. You may also have to put up with competitors' ads appearing in the video player on your site, which is less than ideal. I would strongly advocate that you post your videos onto the web to drive traffic back to your site, but you should either use a 'blank' player or have your own player created by a specialist company with your branding. When you have your own branded TV player you can not only display this on your own site, thus reaffirming your brand and brand message, you can distribute your own embedded code to customers and clients, safe in the knowledge that wherever your branded player goes, it will always display the message about your company or business consistently and with the right brand image.

Fiona Ryder has over 20 years experience in media, film, TV and technology. A former commercials producer, she has spent the last 15 years developing branded digital media TV networks for multinational companies. Her company StreamExchange is an internet broadcasting company helping companies create TV on the web; see www.streamexchange.tv

Day 23

A Brilliant Brand at Every Touch-Point

Throughout this book I've emphasized that your 'brand' is not your logo or your marketing efforts, but everything that people think and feel about you. But how do your customers and potential customers get to think and feel certain things about you? Where do they get all the ideas and emotions (true and false) that play such a powerful role in deciding the fortunes of your business?

The fact is that your set of meanings is generated by people, and filtered by other people, and edited by more, and re-presented to still others, in a host of ways. But no matter how complex the web of communication through which your brand meanings pass before they become embedded in lots of hearts and minds, they all stem from one very simple source — the actual behaviour of your brand itself.

This chapter is about the different opportunities that your brand has to behave towards people; what marketing people call 'customer touch-points'. These touch-points are the places where brands can so dramatically succeed or fail. They matter that much. And they matter simply because at each touch-point your brand has the opportunity to offer a positive, enjoyable, fulfilling, reassuring, pleasant and engaging experience... or to do the opposite.

The trouble is that good and bad experiences do not have equal weight in our psyche. One negative experience can undermine and even undo the benefits of a host of positive ones. This is why you have to monitor (and constantly adjust and 'tune') every single touch-point. Most businesses, frankly, just don't bother to do this, or they have a half-hearted stab at it and fail. Great brands, by contrast, are acutely aware of all their touch-points and they regularly, often obsessively, examine every single one and work hard to ensure that it's a positive one.

I'm writing this chapter in a coffee shop which provides arguably the best coffee of all the well-known chains. Big plus mark. The staff are quite well trained. They are friendly and helpful and positive and fast. Another big plus mark. The shop has constant music playing, but it's quite nice music (in the last ten minutes I've heard Bruce Springsteen, Glen Campbell, Leonard Cohen and Keane) which isn't exactly challenging but at least isn't hideously bland or annoyingly loud. Medium plus mark.

This coffee shop doesn't seem to mind if I sit here working for an hour with one cup of coffee. Big plus mark. **But**. And it's a big but. This place has some of the most unpleasant toilets I've ever seen. They are dirty, scruffy, uncared for and unpleasant. Things are broken. Can it really be that difficult to look after toilets? Massive negative mark.

I still use this coffee shop and will continue to do so, to a point. But the toilet situation is gradually undermining the whole 'brand' for me. There will be a tipping point.

I've mentioned First Direct elsewhere. You know I'm a fan. Why? Because almost all their touch-points are positive ones. Their advertising doesn't offend or embarrass me (so it doesn't undermine my loyalty to the brand). Their customer service on the phone (their most important touch-point of all) has always seemed impeccable to me. Their online offering is highly efficient and nicely presented. It's all good. However, I think they could and should improve the experience in one area: on the High Street. To pay in cheques I have to visit a branch of HSBC which is of course the parent of First Direct. Nothing wrong with that, and not really anything wrong with the HSBC branch experience, except that there isn't any acknowledgement that I'm a First Direct customer, so I don't feel valued at this point. In fact I feel ever so slightly like a second-class citizen here. This is a touch-point at which I don't feel touched, and it's a missed opportunity.

So, touch-points cover the full range of your brand activity, literally everything you do that touches your customer or potential customer, no matter how obliquely. It all matters.

I want you to examine the touch-points of a brand you love, and one that you hate. Then I want you to look closely, honestly and critically at your own. Because if you can improve the ones that are failing and nurture the ones that are succeeding, you'll be actively engaged in creating an ever more positive brand experience for your customers. And that, in turn, will bring you greater brand success.

Brand Builder Workout

First, let's look at a brand that you love. Think through each touch-point listed below and note down how you feel about how the brand behaves in each case. For example, under the 'Advertising' heading make a note about whether their advertising amuses you, annoys you, embarrasses you, and whether it makes you feel more or less positive about the brand. Some of the touch-points I've listed may not be relevant to the brand you're thinking about. And if there other touch-points that that I haven't listed, you can add them below, of course.

Repeat the exercise with a brand that you hate. Doing the exercise may help to answer the all important question of why you hate them.

Loved Brand

General communication

- Advertising: --
- Sponsorship: --
- Direct mail: --
- Letters to you: --

- Answering the phone: _____
- Dealing with your questions: _____

Online experience

- Clear and attractive website: _____
- Easy navigation: _____
- Quality of content: _____

Packaging

- Appealing: _____
- Appropriate (not over-packaged or under-packaged): _____
- Environmentally friendly: _____
- Easy to open: _____
- Easy to reseal or reuse: _____

Branch experience

- Appealing design of store/branch: _____
- Easy to navigate and use: _____
- Approachable/appropriately friendly staff: _____
- Knowledgeable staff: _____
- Cleanliness/tidiness: _____
- Toilets: _____
- Queues/appointments system: _____

Follow-up experience

- Checking on service satisfaction: _____

- Appropriate interval before follow-up $----------$
- Recognition/rewarding of regular customers: $----------$

Complaints

- Openness to criticism and complaints: $----------$
- Clarity and efficiency of complaints process: $----------$

Other touch-points

Hated Brand

General communication

- Advertising: $----------$
- Sponsorship: $----------$
- Direct mail: $----------$
- Letters to you: $----------$
- Answering the phone: $----------$
- Dealing with your questions: $----------$

Online experience

- Clear and attractive website: $----------$
- Easy navigation: $----------$
- Quality of content: $----------$

Packaging

- Appealing: $----------$

- Appropriate (not over-packaged or under-packaged): _____
- Environmentally friendly: _____
- Easy to open: _____
- Easy to reseal or reuse: _____

Branch experience

- Appealing design of store/branch: _____
- Easy to navigate and use: _____
- Approachable/appropriately friendly staff: _____
- Knowledgeable staff: _____
- Cleanliness/tidiness: _____
- Toilets: _____
- Queues/appointments system: _____

Follow-up experience

- Checking on service satisfaction: _____
- Appropriate interval before follow-up _____
- Recognition/rewarding of regular customers: _____

Complaints

- Openness to criticism and complaints: _____
- Clarity and efficiency of complaints process: _____

Other touch-points

Now it's your turn!

My Brand

General communication

- Advertising: _____
- Sponsorship: _____
- Direct mail: _____
- Letters to you: _____
- Answering the phone: _____
- Dealing with your questions: _____

Online experience

- Clear and attractive website: _____
- Easy navigation: _____
- Quality of content: _____

Packaging

- Appealing: _____
- Appropriate (not over-packaged or under-packaged): _____
- Environmentally friendly: _____
- Easy to open: _____
- Easy to reseal or reuse: _____

Branch experience

- Appealing design of store/branch: _____
- Easy to navigate and use: _____
- Approachable/appropriately friendly staff: _____

- Knowledgeable staff: --
- Cleanliness/tidiness: --------------------------------------
- Toilets: --
- Queues/appointments system: ---------------------------------

Follow-up experience

- Checking on service satisfaction: ---------------------------
- Appropriate interval before follow-up ------------------------
- Recognition/rewarding of regular customers: -----------------

Complaints

- Openness to criticism and complaints: -----------------------
- Clarity and efficiency of complaints process: --------------

Other touch-points

REAL BRAND STORY

MR. SITE

Bea Hatherley, co-founder and director of Mr. Site Ltd., shares the story of a brand that arose from one person's need and interest meeting another's technical skills.

The idea for Mr. Site's Takeaway Website first came about in November 2004 when getting a dot com website online was complicated, confusing and costly. At the time, I was a musician looking for a way to get my work online but felt that design companies were overcharging and underdelivering on the websites they were producing. Mr. Site's co-founder, Stuart Spice, was already a web designer by trade and it was whilst I was picking his technical brain that the vision for Takeaway Website was born.

We both felt that the internet should be accessible to everyone — even those with little or no IT experience – and recognized there was a significant gap in the market for an affordable yet professional, jargon free, all-in-one, DIY website creation tool. Fast forward five years and Takeaway Website is the UK's leading website creation tool with over 80,000 customers across the globe.

So, how did we come up with a brand for Mr. Site? Well, I'll be honest — your brand is always going to be a work in progress. Mr. Site has seen many, many changes over the years. Some have been small tweaks here and there, but others have made a massive impact to our image as a whole. First, let me give you some background behind our product, which will help to explain some of our branding decisions.

Takeaway Website is a web-based application that provides consumers and businesses with all the tools needed to create a unique dot com website (e.g. yourname.co.uk) and get it online — all in one, easy-to-use box. From as little as £19.99, it guides users through every stage of the website building process; from choosing a domain name to setting up a secure online shop, picture galleries and blogging forums. To this day, there is still no other retail website creation tool that offers a single solution to website design, hosting, domain registration and e-commerce.

Strangely, the name for the product came before the name of our company. When we sat down and thought about all the different elements of the product itself, we kept coming back to the same point...it's a website in a box. So, it was a website in box that provides everything needed to get online – it was a complete package in a box...a bit like a takeaway? Hang on, a takeaway website! And there the penny dropped; a name that indicates a complete package, ready for anyone to take away and try. Looking back it was quite a logical process and my advice is always to write down the features of your product and put all the pieces together from there.

Next came the name of the company itself. Stuart had some basic ideas for Takeaway Website long before my first discussion with him, but wasn't sure how to execute his plan. He had already thought up the name 'Mr. Site' in 2000 and when he explained it to me, I thought it was a great starting point. We believe our company name reflects one of its most important core values — simplicity — yet, it also suggests there is a person behind the name; an expert helping you through the process.

This is also what inspired the Mr. Site logo — the thought of an 'approachable expert'. Originally, we based our first Mr. Site on a piece of clip art animation; he looked friendly, helpful and confident. Three years later, we went on to redraw him (he was starting be referred to as 'Mr Claw Hands' in the office!) to look more modern but he still had the same Mr. Site feel. The visual side of our brand, for example packaging, website and marketing materials, has also seen some dramatic changes over the years. Over time, we have launched different versions of the product and gained users at a phenomenal rate — and we now truly realize how important a strong and consistent brand it. It groups our Takeaway Website product range together, it represents clearly what we stand for and, most importantly, builds trust and respect for the Mr. Site brand.

In terms of our brand speak, we have also built up a good bank of phrases that clearly communicate what we stand for. Take our strapline, for example: 'Everything you need to get a professional website online'. All our customer communications have remained jargon-free — everything from newsletters, user manuals and the content on our website — and to demonstrate how committed we are to our users, we are continuously reviewing product features to suit their needs and demands.

Mr. Site is also using new social networking methods to interact with users; we recently launched a forum, got ourselves on Twitter and Facebook to provide helpful tips and tricks and we offer users the opportunity to be happy customers on our website and media case studies. We are very proud of our close relationship with customers and aim to deliver on all needs and expectations — it's this that we believe sets us apart from all our competitors.

So, my second piece of advice to you is to always talk to your customers and make sure your brand is saying to them what you think it is saying. Giving them what they need and want will always give your brand the most competitive edge you could possibly ask for.

Day 24

DESIGN MATTERS

Perhaps the simplest piece of advice in this whole book comes down to this: when it comes to design hire a professional designer. Unless you're a designer by profession of course. But even in that case I would generally advise getting another (non-competing) designer to give an objective view of your proposed visual identity.

I think I should clarify my position on design and visual identities (visual identity, or VI, is the posh term for your logo and all the other design bits that go with the logo). My position, which I know designers in the main will contest, is that I do not believe that great branding begins with design. Rather I believe that great branding starts with meaning. But that's not to say that design doesn't matter. Oh, how it matters!

I love design. I hold good designers in great respect and great ones in awe, and so I believe should you. So your brand does not begin and end with the design of your visual identity. Which is why you should never approach a designer until you've sorted out all sorts of strategic issues first, as I hope this book as a whole argues convincingly.

But, but, but: once you have sorted out the strategic stuff (what your brand is for, what you want it to mean, what values it's going to live by, what is its positioning, what is its story, what will it be called) then you **must** go to a professional designer. Because if it's true that good design can't on its own create a great brand, then it's also true that bad design (or lack of design in the real sense of the word, which is just as common a trap) can kill your brand-child at birth. I can't think of a single great brand that doesn't also possess a visual identity which is at the very least half-decently (and certainly professionally) designed.

So why do so many start-ups and small enterprises in general so frequently fail to utilize the power of good design? There are several reasons, all understandable in a sense, but all dangerous, and all to be avoided. Here are some of them.

We are so exposed to design that we have become almost blind to it. Go to any department store, or supermarket, or mall, or walk down any high street, or watch any TV channel, or look at any book, magazine, newspaper, CD cover, or cereal packet. Everything that you see presented to you commercially by any brand of size and substance will have been professionally, thoughtfully, and often cleverly designed. The design may not always appeal to you specifically. The likelihood in this case is that you are not the prime target audience for that product, store, etc. Design is all around us, so we cease to notice it and have no intrinsic sense of its worth or its subtlety and complexity.

In part because of the fact that everything around us in the urban/commercial world is designed, there is a herd instinct which means that much of this design is bland and non-distinctive. We have come to expect banks to have a certain style and approach. We have to come to expect coffee shops to present themselves in certain ways. We expect our loaves of bread or our tins of beans to have a certain look and feel. That's not to say that we can't tell different logos apart from each other. Of course we can. But it does mean that very few brands stand out as truly distinctive visually: and it is very hard for any to be radically different for fear of appearing weird. Brands that go too far beyond our expectations run the risk of being excluded from our consideration altogether. There is something of a double-bind here for small businesses and brands in particular. You don't want to look like everyone else, but you can't afford to be too different. More of that later.

Related to our 'design blindness' is the fact that we very rarely, if ever, analyze our own responses as consumers to a given piece of design. We just respond, and our response gets in the way of us understanding why we are responding. And this too leads us to take design for granted.

Another problem from the point of view of the small business wanting to use design is our assumption that good design is expensive. We tend to see it as an overhead, another expense in starting up our business. Design all too easily gets stuck on the list of expensive things we have to do but have little emotional interest in, like sorting out a broadband contract, or using an accountant.

Alternatively, design gets lumped in with the list of mundane necessities that we need to source, along with staples, box files, an office chair. In fact design frequently doesn't even get a heading of its own on this shopping list. More often than not it is somehow embraced under the heading of 'stationery' or 'business cards'.

Does this really matter, and if so why? Why isn't design just another business consumable? Well, the short answer is that it matters, a lot. Because your visual identity is the visual/visible expression of what your brand means to the world. Because, in a rather obvious way, your logo is the badge by which your brand and its meanings are carried into the world. The logo doesn't 'mean' anything in and of itself but, boy, does it carry the weight of your brand's meaning. And it had better do that well.

The brutal truth is that (although the visual identities of big brands vary enormously in quality and effectiveness) almost the only truly bad logos that I see frequently are those of very small businesses. Small businesses, I'm sorry to say, are by far the most likely members of the bad design rogues gallery. There are the obvious ones: car workshops, hairdressers, some little neighbourhood cafés, some independent shops, some small online businesses, various 'tradesman' businesses from plumbers to builders, and more. All of these appear regularly in the 'bad design' gang. But there are also

surprising members of this dubious club: financial advisers, account-
ants, lawyers and other professional services as well as holiday businesses, charities and others.

So what are they doing wrong, and how can you avoid falling into
the trap? The following is a simple checklist. If you do everything on
this list you stand a very good chance of a very strong visual identity
for your brand.

- Under no circumstances draw your own logo and take it to a
  printer, or anyone else, to 'tidy up'. The result will do nothing but
  damage to your brand.

- Come to terms with the idea that you are going to commission a
  professional designer and look on your visual identity as an investment not an annoying cost.

- Be clear about all the 'strategic' elements of your brand before
  you talk to a designer.

- Look around your locality and in the media, and collect logos,
  some that you find appealing, and some that you dislike or think
  don't work.

- Think about why each has appealed to you (or not) and try to
  make brief notes about each one: why they work or fail, what
  they convey and so on. The idea is not to imitate someone else's
  logo, but to learn from them.

- Now set about finding a designer. Obviously there are numerous
  places to look, from phone books to online searches. My preference, though, would be ask around: ask a local small brand that
  you admire who did their design work. Recommendation counts
  for a lot. Alternatively, go to a local business network and and ask
  for a few names.

- There's no hardline rule about whether to choose a large firm
  or a small one; many very good designers operate as one-person

businesses. But I think it is very important to go to graphic design specialists, as opposed to firms who do design as part of more general activity. For this reason I would generally look for people who specifically call themselves graphic designers rather than advertising agencies, marketing communication companies, marketing consultants or other catch-all titles.

- Lots of designers are generalists (designing everything from leaflets to college prospectuses to websites). Many of them are very good, of course, but I would advise that you are more likely to get excellent logo design from people who specialize in this particular area of design. So look for people who can show you lots of logos and visual identities that they have created for real clients.

- Before you choose a designer, talk to at least three different ones. Part of the key to getting a great result is to find someone who is not only talented and professional but who also has empathy and understanding of your brand.

- Ask each one for at least two clients who you can talk to, and do take the time to call them and ask about their experience of working with this designer.

- Meet each of your shortlisted designers and give them the brief, and take time to talk it through with them to make sure they understand it and to allow them to ask questions.

- Ask each one to come back to you with a costed proposal. Stress that this should be a fully broken-down quotation showing the costs of the initial designs (usually called concepts), then the costs of developing your selected design into a finished logo, then the costs of applying this logo to various uses (signage, letterheads, business cards and so on), and the cost of producing artwork (the digital file which goes to printers).

- **Don't** ask a designer to create any designs as part of their costed proposal. Designers get asked all the time for 'a few rough ideas' but I think this is unfair and unhelpful. You should be able to judge their ability by their previous work, and no-one should expect designers to create anything speculatively.

- Most graphic designers will expect to create two or three concepts for you to consider within the price. Some designers (but not all, make sure you check this) will agree that if you think their concepts miss the mark they will create new design concepts without additional charge. This is a good thing to have in your agreement: and don't be afraid to reject ideas which you are certain are wrong. Equally though, don't abuse this element of your agreement and ask for endless variations because you can't make up your mind.

- When you've chosen your designer make sure that you agree timings as well as costs, including when you will see the first concepts, how long you can 'live with them' before making a decision, when you expect the development work to be completed, when you need artwork and so on.

- If you need things printed, then my advice would always be to put the management of this in the hands of the designer. Professional designers should understand the ins and outs of printing, paper and other factors very well, and they will almost always make better decisions and get a better price for printing than you can. Printing is hugely complex. Leave that to experts: you've got a brand to build!

- Most designers will want to present their concepts to you face to face. That's fine, but remember that if they have to 'sell' an idea to you that might be an indicator that the idea has some problems. Remember your visual identity has to stand on its own merits in the real world. You won't be able to explain it to your customers. If it needs explanation then it's failing as a logo.

- Don't make any decisions in this presentation meeting. Even if you absolutely love or absolutely hate one of the designs you are shown, make sure you can take them away and think about them for several days, or ideally for a couple of weeks. Show them to people who understand what your business is about, and to some people who don't, and get their reactions.

Compare your favourite concept to your original collection of logos that you like and dislike. How does it sit amongst them? Does it fall into the trap of imitation?

By the time you get to this last point above you should have developed a strong working relationship with your designer and you will have a much better understanding of design and its power than most small businesses, which will help your brand enormously.

THE EXPERT VIEW

Top 10 tips on design for small brands

Scott Poulson, Special Design Studio

1. What is a visual identity?

A visual identity is the combination of type, colour and image that will make your brand visually distinctive and announce you to the world. Consistency here is of the utmost importance, it generates recognition so that the public can begin to put their faith and trust in repeated communications from your business. The best way to get a great visual identity is to seek out a good graphic designer.

2. Research

But before you engage with a designer do some homework. You are probably familiar with many of the visual identities within the sector in which you mean to operate. If not, have a good look at them, far and wide, in this country and overseas. This is easy on the web. It will give you a really good idea about what your competitors look like. This will help you distill your ideas about what you like and dislike. Your designer will also go through this process and it will help them to position you in that marketplace whilst differentiating you from your competitors.

3. Why hire a designer?

Designers are experts in visual communications. They work across a great range of media and surfaces producing anything you can think of where image and type need to be applied. You need to hire a designer to help you position your brand in the marketplace.

It is true that modern software has brought desktop publishing within most people's grasp. But just because you have a chisel doesn't mean you are a sculptor. A good graphic designer will have studied the art of composition; will have a passion for typography and knowledge of both current trends and classic styles. They will combine all this with imagination and, in many cases, a style and approach that they have developed over the years.

4. Which designer do you hire?

A recommendation is the best place to start. However, most designers have online portfolios. Look at all their work and think about whether it would meet your needs. Do they have experience in a similar field? Do they have a visual style you can identify with? Look for client recommendations on their website.

Obviously cost is a major factor. Most designers will evaluate your project and quote based on the amount of hours they think it will take. It helps to have a budget in mind for yourself. If you find out you can't afford what they are quoting ask them what they could do within your budget. Failing that, ask them if they can recommend a designer who could work within your budget. Remember that design isn't a commodity; if you shop around on the internet you could get a logo designed for as little as £100, but in the end you get what you pay for.

5. The first meeting

Designers are as individual and as distinctive as their handwriting. Give 100 designers the same brief and you will get 100 different interpretations. You need to use your instincts to find someone on your wavelength. Don't be afraid to talk to several designers in order to find that special spark with someone; it is about trust and understanding. Let's face it, it is your idea and when you express it to a designer read how they react. If they get interested and excited that is obviously a good start. You want them to believe in your business. If they don't, it will show.

6. A visual landscape

The designer will show you their work but a good starting point might be for you to take something visual that you really like, for example other brands' marketing material, pictures, inspiration from magazines, paint swatches, etc. This helps to set a visual landscape, which should inform the work.

7. The brief

The brief is a conversation. Between you and the designer. Pour out all your ideas, what you love, what you hate. What you think you need. Describe your business from top to toe. Be clear about your requirements and expectations and let the designer then make the process clear to you. Recap at the end of the meeting and agree on the outline of the brief, a times-cale and the understanding that a quote will be forthcoming. Expect the designer to formally write up the brief for you both to refer to later on in order to see if the initial requirements are all met.

8. Listen to the expert

After you have agreed to the brief and the initial quote, your designer will proceed. When the designer presents their initial ideas don't discount anything. The best approach is to consider all the routes presented and live with the designs for a while to see how they feel after a few days. First reactions can often be correct but sometimes subtleties in a design may come out in time. Don't forget, they are the expert and often know best! However, you are the client and you will have strong ideas so express your ideas and make suggestions if you need to. Your designer will incorporate them whilst producing their interpretations. Once you have decided on a particular route, the designer will then go away and perfect that version. Keep working together until **you** are happy.

9. Implementation

Once you have chosen your visual identity you will then want to apply it to all your marketing material and get it out there in to the marketplace. Your designer will be able to advise you on what to actually produce for your target market, such as a brochure, catalogue, posters, etc. The designer's job is to make sure this is consistent and free of technical errors. In digital media mistakes can be corrected with the click of a button, but print is fraught with danger. Make sure you proofread everything and get a colleague to do the same before you sign off the final artwork.

10. Staying close

Don't say goodbye once the work is done! A designer should be an integral part of your business. Graphic designers see a lot of businesses and see a lot of people with ideas. They are creative people with active imaginations. A designer may be able to suggest innovations and ideas that could elevate your business idea to an even higher level. And lastly, recommend your designer. Be a champion for them as they are for you.

Scott Poulson founded his graphic design practice Special Design Studio after a career including being a designer for a major publisher and Creative Director at brand and marketing agencies. See more of Scott's work at www. specialdesignstudio.co.uk

Day 25

YOUR PERSONAL BRAND BEHAVIOUR

Warning: here come several statements of the blindingly obvious: Forgive me. We're all different. We're only human. Nobody's perfect Some days we behave and perform better than others.

I can't imagine many folk taking issue with the above, unless it's to question why I'm bothering to state such obvious truths. Well, I'm stating these platitudes about our human frailty because as 'brand owners' we, you and I both, need to come to terms with another rather brutal truth which is: nobody else gives a damn how you feel today.

Well, of course the people who love you care about how you feel. And they will, to a degree at least and from time to time, cut you some slack and forgive you your grumpiness, tardiness, abruptness, forgetfulness, clumsiness, ineptness and doziness. But your customers won't, and indeed shouldn't, forgive any of those things. You will, if you have followed the advice in this book, be well on the way to creating in your customers' minds and hearts a picture of what your brand is, what it means, and what they are entitled to expect from it. If you allow your human frailties, moods, weariness, troubles or anxieties to get between your brand and your customer you can do some significant and lasting damage.

Let me give you some specific examples. Have you ever been in a café, small restaurant, little hotel or bar where you have witnessed the owner-manager admonishing or undermining a junior member of staff? I'm sure you've seen and heard something like that more than once. And what impression does it leave with you? Does it make you think that the owner is passionate about the brand? Are you impressed by the diligence and commitment to customer service that the owner is demonstrating by letting rip at the junior? No, I thought not: much more likely that your sympathies are with the person being told off. We sympathize with the underdog, it's human

nature. Even if we recognize shortcomings in the junior's performance we take no pleasure in those being exposed and criticized in
front of us. Instinctively we know that's not the way to handle staff.
And deep inside we also recognize that the scenario actually demonstrates more about the weaknesses of the brand owner than their
strengths. We suspect that the brand owner has let some personal
factors (maybe just plain old stress) command their behaviour. And
that doesn't make us feel more positive about them or, by association, their brand. Months or even years of positive brand experience
can be undone by the brand owner's behaviour.

And remember it doesn't have to be the actual 'owner' of the business. It could be a member of your senior team undoing all your
hard work.

And it isn't only if you are in 'direct' contact with customers, client or the media that your behaviour matters. Behaviour (from the
things you say to the way you say them, even to the way you close a
door, or the way you breathe) can and definitely does have an effect
on your brand. How? Through the way that your behaviour impacts
on your team.

I've known several businesses where the anxieties and pressures felt
by the owners have had a daily impact on the staff team. The behaviour of these bosses has not always been negative, but it was frequently unpredictable. Predictably unpredictable if you like. And unpredictability can be almost as bad as downright consistent negativity.
You know the scenario. Staff get so attuned to it that they can tell by
the way the boss sighs as they enter a room whether it's going to be
a glass half-full day or a glass half-empty one. And the knowledge
quickly spreads round the office, or the factory, or the restaurant.

"Watch out, he's in a bad mood today," they whisper to each other.
Or, "Blimey, he's very jolly today, wonder what's happened?"

Sure, you're the boss, of course you're going to feel anxious and stressed some of the time. You've got the money worries. You've got the marketing plan to sort out. You've got the new product or service to think through. Or maybe you've just had a bloody great row with your teenage son or with your spouse before you came into the office.

But here's the tough truth. You're the brand owner. In some fancy marketing books you're referred to as the chief brand protagonist. That's a big responsibility. Chief brand protagonist means you are the leading player in the drama that is your brand story. You can not, you must not, ever, let your personal stresses, anxieties, fears or other negative feelings impact on your team, any more than on your customers.

And before we leave the topic, remember that unpredictable 'up' moods are potentially just as damaging. It's when you're over-excited and over-optimistic that you will make the decisions you will later regret. Chasing after unsound opportunities that happen to cross your desk. Or treating a particular member of staff in a way that to others appears to be favouritism. Or setting a precedent by over-servicing a particular client or customer.

I'm not trying to turn you into a robot. I'm not trying to deny your feelings as a human being. In fact, quite the opposite. This book is about the emotional side of branding as much as any other aspect. Brands are about meanings and feelings far more than they are about the rational. But it is precisely for this reason that it so important for you as the brand owner, the brand leader, the chief brand protagonist, to manage your own emotional state when you're in any sense 'on duty' and therefore to ensure that your behaviour adds to your brand's value and doesn't ever-so-gradually, ever-so-poisonously, undermine it.

In the end, in many senses, **you** are your brand. What **you** do **really matters**.

Brand Builder Workout

Here's a checklist you might like to go through to make sure your own behaviour is consistent with your brand promise.

- First, remind yourself here of your brand's values

- Now just remind yourself of your brand positioning statement (and don't be embarrassed, I can't always remember mine.

- Now, with your values and your brand positioning firmly in your mind, think about these aspects of your behaviour and ask yourself if they routinely, or even occasionally, undermine your brand. Be very honest with yourself and consider each question individually for a few moments. Please do write your answers down, no matter how briefly. Writing is 'behaviour' and it is much harder to deceive yourself when you write things down than it is if you just read over the questions and 'think' the answers. Think about:

  - The way you talk to underperforming staff

  - The way you deal with clients/customers/suppliers who need to speak to you unexpectedly

  - The way you handle disappointing news about your business (increased costs, lower than target sales, key member of staff handing in notice)

  - The way you start your day after a less-than-happy breakfast-time (argument or family conflict, or personal 'issues' of any kind)

  - Your response to long-awaited or unexpected good news (contract win, better than predicted financial results, etc.)

  - Your response to an unsolicited 'opportunity' that looks terribly exciting (what my wife calls shiny, pretty things)

  - The way you respond to senior team members who openly disagree with your decisions or opinions

- The emotional signals you give off by the way you smile (or don't) when you first greet people in the morning

- The body language you use when talking face to face to clients, customers, junior and senior staff

- The body language you use when you are on the phone (yes, people can read body language over the phone, because the way you sit, stand or slump affects your tone of voice, your breathing and even the pace at which you speak)

Now, to conclude, ask yourself these few specific and challenging questions. Again, to get the most from this exercise, please do write down your answers.

- Is it true that I sometimes let my anxieties, stresses or just plain bad moods affect the way I deal with staff and/or customers and, if so, how am I going to avoid these negative impacts in the future?

- Is it true that my actual, physical 'tone of voice' sometimes betrays my emotions, either by showing anxiety, anger or gloom or even unexplained optimism or over-excitedness and, if so, how am I going to manage these unintended 'brand messages' in the future?

- Is it true that my non-verbal behaviours (from the way I open and close doors to the way I walk around the office, the way I stand at the window, or the way I sigh or even the way I laugh) betray my inner feelings which may be at odds with the brand messages I actually want to give out and, if so, how can I manage those behaviours in the future?

Your behaviour, of any kind, matters so much to the integrity of your brand. You and your brand are non-different. And that is never truer than for the small brand. I believe that good and great brands are essentially positive and optimistic constructs. In other words, they are created by people who, at least at the moment of the creation, believed that the world is essentially a positive place and that positive outcomes are possible and even likely. And if that's true, then by hook or by crook it is vital for you as the brand leader to maintain that sense of positivity and optimism and to reflect that in your behaviour.

Day 26

HOW TO GET YOUR STAFF TO LIVE YOUR BRAND

Anyone can tell an employee to 'live the brand', because words are cheap. But actually developing fierce brand loyalty and brand-building behaviour in your staff team is another matter altogether. The great brands manage it, and they don't necessarily do it by paying higher wages or by putting fresh fruit on the meeting room table.

Fundamentally, getting your staff to believe in your brand as much as you do is about authentic engagement coupled with genuine empowerment. They aren't difficult as concepts, but in my experience they are quite challenging for many entrepreneurs to do well.

Entrepreneurship is a kind of spirit, a state of mind, perhaps even a personality type. As such it has some very powerful, positive and distinctive characteristics.

Entrepreneurs in my experience have a tendency to be:

- Interested in big ideas

- Passionate about their values

- Always wanting to move forward

- Intuitive

- Brave

- Energetic

- Charismatic

- Inspiring

These are all positives, or at least they contain the potential for hugely positive action and achievement. That's what makes entrepreneurs special. That's what makes people like you and I want to start businesses, and to sacrifice the 'security' of a 'job' in favour of the apparent risks of running our own show. However, there is a downside (which some might even call a dark side). Entrepreneurs sometimes also exhibit these tendencies:

- Lack of interest in practical details

- Over-interest in practical details (sometimes randomly and un-predictably)

- Emotional unpredictability (today ecstatically upbeat, tomorrow full of doom and gloom)

- Surprisingly lacking in intuition about what others in their team are thinking or feeling

- Suddenly and surprisingly over-cautious

- Suddenly and surprisingly enthusiastic about a completely new project which no-one else in the team knows about

- Bullish and bullying

- Inclined to favouritism

- Impulsive

I could go on. Honest entrepreneurs reading this book will recognize both these sets of characteristics, I hope: and it's in the gap between them where lies the problem of staff engagement with your brand.

The brutal truth is that nobody (honestly, nobody) cares about your brand as much as you do. You simply have to come to terms with that in order to move on to authentic staff engagement.

That's not to say that your team can't or won't become passion-ate advocates, supporters and ambassadors for the brand. Of course they can. But by acknowledging the reality of the situation you will be able to move forward from a solid starting point. To do otherwise will inevitably result in the disappointment, bitterness and dark emotional responses which so many entrepreneurs allow themselves to slide into.

So the truth is: your staff members are another audience for your brand, just as your customers and potential customers are. Just as the media are. Just as your bank manager is.

With this in mind you need to think about how you communicate with them, regardless of whether there are a handful (or fewer) of them, or whether you employ tens or even hundreds of people.

Years ago I carried out a consultancy project for an industrial company. The firm wanted to know why productivity appeared to be decreasing even though there was a financially-based 'incentive' scheme in place which was intended to motivate workers to be more productive.

I spent several days on several different sites talking to a substantial sample of the workforce. I discovered a very simple answer to the company's question. The workers felt that the company did not communicate with them 'properly' and as a consequence they felt strongly that the company and its senior managers held them in 'contempt'.

I didn't choose the word 'contempt'. That's the word that several workers used.

On closer examination I found that all these staff wanted was to be treated with respect, to be communicated with as adults, and to be treated fairly and honestly by their employer. Much to my surprise there was a deep well of good will towards the company, pride in its work, and a preparedness to support 'the brand'. But all that good will, all that latent positive brand engagement, was suppressed and wasted by the lack of engagement and lack of 'authenticity' of the senior managers and of the company's head.

The lesson here is not complex, but it requires some discipline on the part of the entrepreneur. This is not a book about leadership or even about management, but it's when you are dealing with the brand engagement of your staff that the fine art of leadership meets the craft of branding.

Here are my simple rules for the successful brand engagement of your staff team.

Talk: The key is to communicate often, actively and meaningfully. The more you tell people about what is going on (and importantly 'why') the more engaged they will be. Depending on the size and nature of your company your methods of communication will vary. But much better to be frequent and up to date than less so.

Listen: Communication should go both ways. Ask your people what they think before you make the big decisions! This is not an abdication of your entrepreneurial authority, but a proper balance to your urge towards impulsive action.

Empower: If you want your people to believe in your brand and to act as though it means something to them, then you have to give them some 'ownership' of it. This means you **must** allow them the freedom to plan and to act, resisting the urge to interfere or micro-manage every detail of their work. In other words you **must** release some of your control of your brand. Your job is to tell the brand story to your people effectively, so that they know what to to do and how to behave, not to be on their backs all the time (torturing your-self with the masochistic belief that nobody understands or cares as much as you do).

Respect: Understand that your team are thinking, feeling and able people. Too many entrepreneurs let that thought slip away, both when they are either over-enthused about a new idea (in which case they can march through their own company demanding un-thinking loyalty and excitement from all), and when they are worried or gloomy about some issue or other (in which case they can be seen brooding in corridors or bawling people out in open-plan offices). Neither of these behaviours encourage brand engagement, and both stem from lack of respect.

You'll notice there are no fancy incentive schemes in this list, or reward schemes, or banners hanging from the ceiling, or 'employee of the month' awards. You can do those if you like, and some of them might help, but they will only help if you have the four key elements in place: **talk, listen, empower, respect**.

Brand Builder Workout

Today's task is to audit your brand engagement with your team, using the four simple elements.

Talk: Think about the frequency and regularity with which you communicate with your team. Think about all the ways that you do this (or could do it), including face-to-face briefings, simple conversation, presentations, newsletters and so on. Think about which of your communications are responded to positively or with apparent indifference. What's working? What's missing? Ask them.

Listen: Think about the degree to which you actually listen to members of your team. I mean listen as opposed to tell. Should you, and how can you, increase your opportunities to listen, both formally and informally, one to one and in a group? And think about how you might listen to those in your team who are less inclined to speak to you. Remember, just because they're not speaking to you it doesn't follow that they're happy, or that they aren't speaking (or grumbling) to others.

Empower: Think about the degree of empowerment that your staff have at various levels in your organization. How could you give each person more responsibility for their 'brand behaviour'? You might find it frees your time as well as improving their degree of empowerment.

Respect: This one is the real toughie. Think honestly about your relationships with your staff. Are they really based on simple respect? If you have any doubts, please think carefully about how those relationships impact on your brand, through their impact on staff behaviour and attitude.

THE EXPERT VIEW

Engaging Staff with the Emotional Economy

Caroline Rust, The Coaching Works!

Today's economy is an emotional one. Never since the emergence of consumerism have we been more encouraged and prompted to make buying decisions based upon how we 'feel' about what we buy and who from.

There are countless examples of brands which are marketed to do exactly that: change how we feel about ourselves and the humdrum of our lives. However, what is also apparent is the enormous impact (positive and negative) that those who are personally delivering (or selling) the service or product have on the overall brand experience.

The bottom line is that the people within any business are the embodiment (or they should be) of the brand which they represent. Why spend millions of pounds on clever marketing when it can so easily be negated in a few careless moments by an individual who really couldn't give two hoots about you or your purchase?

So if how who we buy from has such a powerful effect on consumers, how can businesses be certain that they have the right people selling the right products?

Lately, there's been a lot of talk and hype about 'staff engagement'. The popularity of finding ways to engage staff seems to have hit an all-time high. It's a fact that employers want their staff to do their best, not just now and then, but **all** of the time. The truth is that, unlike robots, the human condition means that sometimes we feel more like 'playing' than at others. And when employees decide to play more than focus on the task in hand, then trouble is often in store.

The bottom line is that employees want work, stimulating jobs which are worthwhile, and they want to feel valued and respected by their employers. Clever employers are looking to find ways to seek out a win-win solution that meets both their commercial needs and those of their employees.

Ultimately this challenge is both a subjective and objective one and it cannot begin until firstly the business is crystal clear about its own brand values. Thereafter, seeking ways to express and embed these values to the employee and the customer is the next step and it's not about clever buzz words and posters in the staff restaurant.

I've worked with numerous MDs, CEOs and HR Directors who have told me they want staff to give them feedback, to play a role in developing the business and challenge the status quo when what their behaviours communicate is 'do what I want and how I want it'.

If we are to inspire employees to want to live the brand, we need to ensure we have the right people at the top of the business (and throughout) who also understand and demonstrate that.

Having a workforce that goes beyond what is expected is rare. If engagement is the total of a person's loyalty, hard work and ability to support and work with colleagues, then maybe these are the qualities that should be apparent around the board table. In my experience, the members of most boardrooms often need to be reminded to look at how engaged they themselves are with the workforce. The old adage of 'staff will treat customers equally as well as they themselves are treated' has a lot of truth in it.

Encouraging staff to become a living expression of a brand's values goes beyond the sole task of motivation. Engagement is something that the employee has to offer on their own terms and its origins begin at the very start of the recruitment process. Employers need to remember that every time they deliver on their promises commitments and fulfill their employees' expectations it can only serve to reinforce the employees' sense of trust. Employers need to spend more time listening to their workforce and less time telling them to 'feel happier/more motivated'. Instead they need to encourage, promote and support staff to become engaged with the business.

Employers need to develop proper engagement programmes which **everyone** within the business takes part in. The purpose of such programmes is to get people at all levels involved and immersed with the business and the brand. Simply telling people what the brand values are is not enough – remember posters are simply signposts.

The next time you walk around a department store, look for the clues of who you think has engaged with their brand and who hasn't. Who appears to be a living extension of their brand (and who doesn't)? Ask yourself how do you know? What judgements are you making? What do you notice about people who are fired up, bright eyed and enthusiast? How do they behave, what do they say and what actions do they take? The next time you interview someone, forget the theory and testing for what they know and the words they say; instead listen out for clues as to how they make **you** feel. Recruit for one thing only – 'attitude' – and train for everything else.

Caroline Rust has two decades' experience in media, sales training and recruitment marketing, including having been a Regional Agency Director for Euro RSCG Riley. Now an independent trainer and coach and owner of WorkShopsWork, Caroline provides bespoke development programmes to public and commercial organizations. Find out more at www.workshopswork.co.uk

Day 27

WHY CHEAPER ISN'T ALWAYS BETTER

In the consumer society we are obsessed with price: all our transactions seem to be measured by 'price'. We are surrounded by savings, sales, discounts, special offers, bargains, and deals. If you based your thinking about price purely on a casual observation of your local high street, or by flicking through any newspaper or watching any commercial break on TV, you would quickly come to the (erroneous) conclusion that 'price' is the one and only measure of 'value'.

From that conclusion you might be tempted to jump to another (also erroneous): that it is intrinsically more attractive to your customers for your product or service to be as cheap as possible. It's a mistake, and a big one, which small business owners make frequently.

In the simplest and crudest of scenarios, it may be true that if there are, say, two vegetable stalls next to each other in a market and one is selling its large cauliflowers for £1.00 each whilst the other is selling them at 80 pence each, then the stallholder offering the 80 pence deal will sell out of cauliflowers first. It may be true. But actually, it may not be, even in this uncluttered comparison. Because, in reality, there are always other elements at play.

First, for the direct price comparison to work the vegetables not only to have to be of virtually identical size and quality, but they also have to appear so. So the 80 pence stallholder had better make sure her cauliflowers are just as clean and as attractively presented as her 20% more expensive competitor. And while she's at it she had better ensure that her price tickets are clear and attractive, and that her other products are also cheaper, like for like. If she achieves all this and can put up a sign saying 'cheapest veg on the market' then maybe price will win her more customers than the chap next door. But she's unlikely to do this, because in this scenario with many suppliers competing side by side, as in a town market place, undercutting the competition on price will be seen as cheating by other stallholders and make the undercutter singularly unpopular.

The social mores and peer pressures of market traders aside, simply lowering prices as a strategy for business success is almost certainly doomed to failure in the long run. Imagine you can put up with the mutterings of your fellow stallholders and you boldly go ahead and undercut the going rate for cauliflowers.

A couple of important things have happened. First, you've lowered your profit margin, so to bring in the same amount of sales revenue you have to sell more cauliflowers. We don't need to go into how many more caulis in order to make the point. It's not the detailed maths that matters here. It's the principle. The second thing that has happened is that you have changed customer perceptions of your stall. If you've communicated effectively that you are 20% cheaper than anyone else for a range of popular veg, then don't be too quick to pat yourself on the back. In a sense you've achieved what you set out to achieve, but actually you have just very cleverly undermined your brand.

Now your important story isn't that you are the nice vegetable stall, or the high quality vegetable stall, or the vegetable stall with the widest range. Now, you are 'the cheap vegetable' stall. You've just moved your brand position. If you are happy in that position and you can sustain it by sourcing lower cost vegetables or cutting your costs in other ways (perhaps by deciding not to hire the extra help on a Saturday that you were thinking about), then that's fine. There is nothing wrong in adopting a brand position of 'cheap' as long as you do it intentionally and deliberately. But please don't fall into the trap of ending up in this position by accident.

There are a couple of other important effects of cutting prices like the cauliflower seller. For one thing, it won't be long before your fellow stallholders decide to teach you a lesson, perhaps by working together to do a great deal with a cauliflower supplier (without you) which means they can halve the cost of their cauliflowers. They don't need to do it for long. Just long enough perhaps, to steal back all your price-sensitive customers and critically wound your business. For another thing, remember that your assumption that veg shoppers will always seek out the cheapest cauliflower may be completely illusory. Yes they will save 20% per cauliflower. But is that enough to tempt them? Will they notice? Will they care? Or will they, which could really give you a nasty surprise, assume that your cauliflowers must be in some way inferior to others. They must be, mustn't they? After all, they're 20% cheaper.

And my final dark warning about pricing cheap is this: it's a really difficult position to come back from. What are the vegetable shoppers going to think, once they've got used to you being the cheapest veg stall in town, when you suddenly (or even gradually) try to pull prices back up again? They're not going to like it, at all.

Remember that shoppers in any market place (and I don't just mean the vegetable market) are hugely emotional and sensual. We buy not with our rationality and our intellect, but with our eyes, noses, hands and hearts. Cheaper is not always better: and in fact sometimes unfeasibly expensive is much more appealing to customers.

But in case you have any doubts and are still concerned that cheapest possible price brings maximum possible returns, let me give you a couple of examples. Starting with the kings of cheap on the High Street: Poundland. At the time of writing, in the summer of 2009, British retailer Poundland is riding high (alongside several other retailers who have built their brands on the premise of being extraordinary value). But therein lies the key to their success. Their blunt brand-name notwithstanding, Poundland is not actually about 'cheapness' but about 'value'. Because the brilliance of the Poundland offering is that a substantial proportion of their product range actually consists of branded goods which customers recognize and trust — but offered at almost staggeringly low prices. Ten Philips low energy lightbulbs for £1.00. One hundred Tetley teabags for £1.00. Twelve Kodak batteries for £1.00. And so on.

Low prices works for Poundland because of the effort they put into their buying, and because they have created a brand that is powerful enough to persuade producers of branded goods from Cadbury to Kelloggs to supply them, and in some cases to supply special pack sizes to fit into Poundland's fixed-price positioning. Maxwell House is just one example, producing a 100g coffee jar specially for Poundland.

But before we all get carried away with the idea of opening an Eightypenceland remember the point: for Poundland, low price is a conscious positioning that they have made into a core brand promise.

And to give a completely contrasting example to Poundland, I'll tell you a little about my own business. It's a contrast most notably because I don't sell any products (well, apart from this book), but also because of my price positioning.

What I sell, as consultant/advisor/speaker is probably more accurately described as a service than a product. I do stuff for client organizations, although that stuff often takes the form of me speaking about things, thinking about things, then speaking about things some more. The idea, of course, is to make some kind of substantial improvement to the client's business or organization; usually in the arena of their brand and their branding activity, though sometimes connected to more general business strategy or the development of their senior people.

The big challenge for me in pricing, and it's a challenge faced by thousands of people who would broadly describe themselves as 'consultants' of one kind or another, lies in establishing an appropriate price for this rather intangible work that we do.

There is a school of thought, one that you can find in a number of books about running your own business or becoming a consultant, that tries to tackle this question from the costs end of the equation. In other words, pricing for your service is based on what you need to earn in order to pay all your bills and leave you with some kind of surplus (variable depending on your desired lifestyle, I suppose). This method at first appears to be rather neat, but it has a huge flaw in it, into which it is all too easy to fall.

Assume that you calculate that in order to live a reasonably comfortable life you need to make sales of say £60,000 per year, because it costs £10,000 per year to run your business, leaving you with profit of £50,000. Forget about tax and so on, and don't take these specific figures literally: it's only an illustration of a principle. And let's assume that you are planning to work on average for 45 weeks of the year. Roughly speaking, you will therefore need to be generating sales of £1333 per week (£60,000 divided by 45 weeks). How many days do you want to sell each week? Not five, I hope. That will be virtually impossible, unless you want to do all the other tasks (like building your brand) at the weekend or in the evenings. Let's say you want to sell three days of your precious time each week. What is your time worth? Well, according to this ghastly method you have just priced yourself at £444 per day.

That's pretty damn close to where I started when I first ventured into the world of consulting, and it's been a long hard struggle (and one involving a substantial repositioning job on my part) to move away from this. What's wrong with it (you might be thinking) — £444 isn't a bad wage in anyone's book, is it?

Whilst the actual figure is a subjective thing, a matter of opinion, a matter of what you want from your business, it's the principle of how we got to this figure which is so dangerous from a brand perspective. Because this figure is an indicator of the production cost to you, not of the value to the customer. And because of that it is as much a trap as that of dropping the prices of your cauliflowers.

Once you tell the world that you charge £444 per day as a consultant (oh all right, let's be really bold and go for £500), then you have not just made a statement about your price but also about your value. Imagine that you are a director of a major company looking for a consultant to help with a particularly thorny strategic issue, in whatever area. Imagine that you ask for proposals from three consultants whose names you have been given by your PA or an executive who has done a bit of research.

Imagine that one of these consultants says that the project is likely to take 10 days, and at his day rate of £500 per day the total cost will be £5000. You've never heard of this consultant before, but he looks quite professional, and he's cheap. He says in his proposal that if the project takes a bit longer than anticipated he will charge you an additional day rate of £300 per day. So if it takes 12 days instead of 10 you will pay £5600.

Consultant two, of whom you are vaguely aware via a colleague, is more expensive at £750 per day, but believes that the project can be completed in 8 days, bringing the total fee to £6000 (20% higher than the first). But at least you've heard of this guy. And this guy is also bold enough to say his quote is a fixed one. If it takes a day or two longer then he doesn't charge any more. This guy looks good value.

Consultant three appears not to have a day rate, or at least doesn't quote one. In fact she asks you for an estimate of the value of the project to you in terms of how much the company would be improved by successful implementation of the project. You acknowledge that this project is pretty important. In fact it could bring savings of £240,000 over the coming two years. This third consultant responds with a short but comprehensive proposal, concluding with a fixed price for the project of £12,000. In other words, she wants to charge you 5% of your potential savings. That's twice as expensive as the second consultant. Outrageous, isn't it? But you ask around a bit. This consultant has a strong reputation. She is actually known to be more expensive than most.

In fact she isn't just 'more expensive' she is 'at the top end of her profession'. She doesn't measure her value by the hour but by the value of her input. She seems to think that she is worth every penny. You're intrigued. Other people say she is highly effective.

Perhaps £12,000 is actually good value when you consider the value of the project's successful conclusion to the company. Isn't it better to pay a bit more upfront for a better result? And nobody is going to thank you for hiring either of the cheaper consultants if it all goes wrong. In fact, if it did go wrong then at least you could say you went for the highest quality option. And, when push comes to shove, aren't you somewhat reassured and more confident in the project because you know you've hired the best?

See what I mean? Cheapest is not always best. Sometimes expensive is best. And to add icing to the cake, with her value-based pricing approach, the third consultant in our story can afford to have less client-contact time (i.e. sell fewer days), giving herself time to do more brand work, more study to improve her work, and more interesting activities to help make her a more interesting and fulfilled individual who becomes even more persuasive in client meetings. For her higher pricing is a win-win: building her brand reputation just as it builds her income.

All industries and market sectors are different, as are all individual businesses. There is no golden rule for pricing, as I hope you can tell from the above. The trick is to ask yourself some key questions before deciding: and to remember that we are in the business here of building a powerful, positive and sustainable brand, as opposed to that of selling lots of product at the lowest possible price.

Brand Builder Workout

1. **Do I have much choice over my pricing anyway or is it dictated by the market for my particular product or service?** If the answer to this is 'no' then my best advice is to be 'competitive' in pricing (i.e. on a par with others) and to concentrate on other aspects of your brand to drive your sales up (better quality, better service, better relationships with customers, better stories).

2. **If there is room for movement on price and do I want to go up or down compared with competitors?** Only you can decide this, but just make sure it's a conscious choice. If you want to go lower then that's fine, but make it a brand decision like Poundland. Offer real value advantages. If you want to go higher then ensure that there is added value for the customer. Your coffee may be fundamentally the same as the cheap coffee shop on the corner, but maybe you can offer a nicer, more interesting ambience.

3. **Have you arrived at your price according to a calculation based on cost of production to you or value to the customer?** Looking at pricing from the perspective of value to the customer is always the preferable approach. And it's an approach that still works even if you're a hairdresser as opposed to a consultant. Two hairdressers in my home town have two completely different approaches to pricing. One charges about £12 for a man's haircut. It's a perfectly serviceable haircut, carried out by nice people in a nice, jolly, friendly environment. Sometimes you have to sit and wait for half an hour if it's busy. Another hairdresser charges £27 for essentially the same service. Though that includes washing as well as cutting. And you get a cup of coffee.

    More importantly, the offering is just a little more sophisticated, the haircutting a little more professional. The whole experience a bit more... special. The expensive hairdresser knows that many people would say it was too expensive, but it's fine with that, and there is no shortage of customers. Its particular customers are prepared to pay more for a different kind of service and this business has priced itself accordingly, not according to cost of production, but according to value to the customer. Their customers wouldn't want to pay any less.

4. **Does your pricing policy support and enhance or undermine your brand ambitions?** Try to look at your brand from the outside. Is it right for it to be cheap, or would more expensive just 'feel' better? Only you can decide, but at all costs resist the temptation to buy your way into the market by cutting the price of your cauliflowers.

Day 28

What to Do When Your Brand Gets Things Wrong

Every business lets down its customers now and again. Nobody is immune. You will disappoint someone soon. Don't be down-hearted by this. We're all only human. The important thing is to have a strategy in advance which will enable you to respond most appropriately when things do go wrong. It's how well (and how fast) you respond that counts.

This (short) chapter explains what to do when things go wrong, and just as importantly **when** to do it. A simple checklist which can be referred to when the going gets rough: and which can actually turn potential disaster into a **win**, creating stronger brand advocates than you ever had before.

Have you ever been treated less than satisfactorily in a shop, or on the phone, or in a restaurant? Or have you ever bought a product or a service that has left you feeling underwhelmed, disappointed, or downright 'had'? Of course you have. I've never met anyone who hasn't had that experience numerous times. Even the finest brands with the best products, top service and great customer-service training, sometimes let you down.

Brand Builder Workout

Here's an uncomfortable exercise. Take a moment now to think of all the ways that your business could potentially 'let down' your customer. They will probably fall under the following headings (and I've suggested a few possible specifics under each heading – be honest, do any of these apply to you?). And remember, being 'let down' is a matter of perception. It doesn't matter what you as the business owner thinks: it's what your customer or potential customer thinks that's important here.

Price disappointment

- it's cheaper elsewhere
- it just seems really expensive

- it was in the sale last week and now it's gone up again

- it was full price when they bought it, and a week later it's much cheaper in the sale

- there's such a big discount when buying two or three that I feel punished for buying just one

Value disappointment

- it just doesn't seem big/good/stylish/attractive/distinct/desirable enough for the price being charged

- it feels like I'm being charged more just because I'm a captive audience in this cinema/theme-park/service-station/village/airport

- I was given the impression that I would receive a host of benefits which have not amounted to very much

Availability disappointment

- it's never open when I need it to be

- they are always 'experiencing a particularly high volume of calls'

- the specific product isn't available (at least not at that price)

- I can't find the phone number on the website

Communication disappointment

- they say they will call back (they don't)

- they have mislaid my letter (at least they say they have, though I don't believe them)

- they never answer the bloody phone!

- the phone is answered by an automated system and I have to go through five layers of selecting options before I get put on hold because they are 'experiencing a particularly high volume of calls'!

Attitude disappointment

- the assistant is surly or uninterested
- the agent is abrupt and patronising
- the manager just doesn't seem to care about me or my problem
- a simple smile or some warmth seems too much to ask
- (by contrast) the assistant is fawning and over-familiar
- the assistant calls me 'mate' (bizarrely I was once called 'chap' as in "can I help you chap?" by a clothes-shop assistant who had clearly been given not even the most cursory briefing on how to talk to customers)

Efficiency disappointment

- the product just doesn't do what they said it would
- the service just doesn't do what they said it would
- I've been sitting at this table for 15 minutes and haven't got a menu yet
- all our meals arrived at different times (which is only acceptable in the excellent Wagamama's where they make a brand-virtue of it)
- they promised fast delivery but it's been a couple of weeks now

Et cetera, et cetera.

Now have a think about how your business could let down your 'potential' customer, or even those who may not become customers personally but who may influence others (journalists, for example, or just people who talk to other people!)

Reputation disappointment

- I keep reading or hearing less than enthusiastic reports about them. (Example: there's a restaurant in my home city about which people routinely say, "it's very nice, so long as you're not in any kind of hurry", and it's not intended as a compliment. The funny thing about this example is that it has become a cliché which has spread far and wide. It may not be fair, but it is now part of the brand reputation. In other words it's a disappointment 'before the fact'.)

- They used to be really good, but I keep hearing that they've lost the plot a little (and as Tesco's know... every 'little' helps, or hurts)

Visual disappointment

- the logo is ugly, the shop front is ugly, the website is ugly, the business card is ugly (I'm using the word ugly broadly here: it may just be not very beautiful)

Verbal disappointment

- I don't like the way their advertising shouts, simpers, play-acts, over-promises

Communications disappointment

- Why won't they answer my perfectly reasonable questions?

And so on and so forth. The list of potential ways to disappoint a customer is potentially a very long one. If you were honest, and I'm sure you were, I'm guessing that you've built up quite a list yourself. But this exercise wasn't intended to depress you: rather to demonstrate that there are so many potential vulnerabilities in your efforts to please your customers that you really cannot guarantee that you will never let them down. In fact, I think you can pretty much guarantee that you will.

So what can any of us do about that? Well, it's a matter of doing everything positive to get things right whilst knowing precisely what to do when things go wrong. And that isn't complicated, frankly. In fact, it really comes down to one simple little word.

You guessed it: SORRY.

Such a simple word. With such power. And yet fraught with so many dangers. Contrary to Elton John, or rather to Bernie Taupin, I don't think that sorry is always the hardest word to say. In fact I think the problem lies in the ease with which some people and organizations say 'sorry'. It is frequently said dismissively, or insincerely, or utterly impersonally via some pompous inactive phrase such as 'with regret' or 'unfortunately on this occasion. . .'.

Sometimes, of course, businesses either refuse to say 'sorry' or they just don't seem to realise that an apology is not only appropriate but goes a very long way to making things better. So my absolute rule number one when things go wrong, when a customer or potential customer expresses any kind of dissatisfaction or displeasure at all, is an immediate, sincere, personal, unqualified and active apology.

Immediate: The time to apologize is right now. Don't wait to investigate circumstances or facts. If your customer is unhappy, apologize right now (or sooner).

Sincere: Customers, especially disappointed ones, can detect insincerity through special sensors which grow larger and more powerful in the course of being disappointed (well not really, but you know what I mean). So you **must** be sincere. And if you're wondering "how do I fake sincerity?" then you've missed the point. You can't fake sincerity, but you shouldn't have to once you commit to the fundamental truth that to your business your customer's unhappiness is sincerely threatening.

Don't apologize to your customer as a chore. Apologize because you sincerely understand that your customer is the single most important element in making your brand successful. I won't trot out the cliché about a happy customer telling X number of customers and an unhappy one telling XXX more. It's an utterly unproven and unprovable statistic. It may not be true at all, in fact: but frankly it doesn't matter if your unhappy customer doesn't tell anybody. The point is that by accepting an unhappy customer as a normal part of business and therefore underestimating the need to apologize, you have subtly but surely undermined your brand.

Personal: Your brand might be a 'concept' or a 'construct' but it should behave like a person (and a nice one into the bargain), and that person (at least when you're a small organization) is **you**. So when you apologize do so as an individual. Say "I'm sorry" not "we regret". And the personal touch works both ways. Treat the customer as the individual that they are. Avoid standard letters at all costs. Write something short but fresh every time. Refer to their specific problem to prove that you understand their particular story and concerns. Sign it personally. And give them a number where they can contact you easily and personally.

Unqualified: When you are telling your children how much you love them, do you qualify it with a brief résumé of how they might improve so that you'll love them even more? Of course not. When you are comforting someone you love who is distressed, do you comment reasonably that they brought this sad situation upon themselves? I hope not. And when you apologize to a customer, avoid the temptation, no matter how great, to qualify that apology with an analysis of their contribution to the problem.

A qualified apology is no apology at all. I'm not talking here about legal situations to do with liability and so on. Sure there are special considerations if you're in legal dispute with someone (or likely to become so). But let's be realistic; most unhappy customers aren't about to sue you. Most of them just want you to say you're sorry (because we all have a need to be acknowledged as human beings with feelings) and for you to do something to correct the situation.

Active: The final vital facet of a convincing apology is for it to be active. This means two things. First, that the voice is active: that your apology sounds like it comes from a real, sentient, feeling person and not from a computer. Second, that the apology is in a sense a living, breathing thing that has a life beyond the actual letter or phone call (never, by the way, apologize by email). In other words the apology should not end with the words but must convey a real sense that you are going to do something which will redress things.

Maybe it is beyond your power to undo the perceived wrong. But it must be within your power to do something positive or rewarding for the customer which they will clearly perceive as you bringing your apology to life. Furthermore, if you convincingly explain the steps you have taken to ensure that the disappointment won't happen to anyone else in the future then this can be a deeply satisfying and ameliorative result for the customer. And that is the result you are after. A result which can be summed up in one wonderful word: **forgiveness**.

This is the magic of the proper apology. Proper forgiveness. And from proper forgiveness you can turn an unhappy customer into a new advocate for your brand. I know this because I've experienced it from both ends (both as unhappy customer and apologetic brand protagonist).

Can it really be that simple? Is that all you have to do when things go wrong? Well, almost. To be honest, the apology business is so important in a brand sense, and so easy to get wrong, that putting your efforts into getting that right will put your brand way ahead of most when it comes to unhappy customers.

Having said that, what I recommend is following up the external activity (the Immediate, Sincere, Personal, Unqualified and Active

sorry) with some internal activity. But do them second, only after you've done the apology.

I suggest:

- *Find out* what happened. The actual facts. Not the stories/ interpretations/blaming/excuses. Just the facts and the circumstances.

- *Work out*, with the relevant members of your team, whether processes or any other aspect of your brand behaviour need to change.

- *Agree* the changes with your team and communicate them clearly and incontrovertibly to all concerned (not forgetting to tell your customer – remember it's part of the healing process).

- *Implement* the changes.

This is not a book about customer service, or what corporates are tending these days to call customer experience: but both service and experience are of course a key part of your brand. I don't want you to obsess about things going wrong. But just remember that the most powerful weapon in your armoury when they do is the big fat **sorry**.

Day 29

Brand Extension: Opportunities and Dangers

When a brand is established and showing signs of success (or, indeed, if it is struggling), many people start to dream up new brands, sub-brands and brand extensions. If we make a great bicycle, they think, shouldn't we make great sunglasses too? NOT NECESSARILY! This cautionary chapter is my attempt to save the over-enthusiastic entrepreneur from wasting money and damaging their existing brand by diving into reckless brand extensions.

The phrase 'brand extension' describes the phenomenon when a brand successful in one arena takes its brand name into another. We'll look at several examples. It can be brilliantly successful, of course, making fantastic use of the power inherent in a successful brand to conquer new territories. It can actually even enhance the original brand. But it can also go very wrong.

The really simple rule of thumb when you're thinking about extending your brand is this: will it make sense to the customer? To put it another way, will the customer either understand (intellectually) or feel (emotionally) that there is a real connection between the two products that bear the same brand name?

The Polo brand from Ralph Lauren successfully made the jump from clothing to home furnishings. You can see the connections: linen, comfort, a kind of New England style. The Arm & Hammer toothpaste brand was a natural extension of the same brand's baking soda product. Virgin is one of the greatest of brand extenders: from music to airlines, from credit cards to digital media. Sometimes the connections are tenuous and not all of the brand extensions have been a success. Virgin Cola is no longer with us. But where Virgin have succeeded you can see the connection in 'attitude' rather than in a more tangible link. Credit cards for young spenders who aren't attracted to 'establishment' banks. An trans-Atlantic airline which promises an experience quite different in attitude to the more conventional providers. And so on.

Brand extension is used all the time as a method of 'protecting' new products in a ruthless marketplace where anonymity can mean quick death. A successful brand extension means you are no longer starting from scratch. It has many positives as a strategy. So why am I so cautious? Fundamentally because not only is it a fast track to launching a new product or service in a new sector, but because it can also be a very quick way to damage all the good work you've done in creating your original brand in the first place. A dodgy brand extension can do you harm!

Of course if you're big and highly resourced, and have a reputation for innovation, then a failed brand extension won't damage your core brand (Virgin has survived numerous failed extensions), but if you're a small business nurturing a precious small brand, please be careful about extending it recklessly.

One of the most famous of all brand extension flops was Coca Cola's introduction of 'New Coke' in 1985. A quarter of a century later this embarrassing failure continues to be recounted and must have done the company untold financial damage in terms of lost sales over the years. Of course the company has successfully introduced other extensions, of several different kinds, but it's never ever tried to 'replace' its original product as it did in 1985.

BIC Pens tried to produce BIC tights and stockings – the link was disposability. BIC pens are used and thrown away. As are BIC disposable razors. Same for the tights, went the theory. Women didn't want them. There seemed to be a logical connection, but there wasn't any kind of emotional one.

Some recent brand extension successes include pet-food producer Iams launching pet insurance (see the clear logical/emotional connection?), Starbucks launching a coffee liqueur, and National

Geographic cleverly partnering with Google Earth to give the long-established National Geographic brand a whole new lease of life.

By contrast, nobody really wanted Harley-Davidson's cake decorating kits! Or Colgate ready-meals. Or bicycles from Smith & Wesson (yes, the gun manufacturer). Or Cosmopolitan (the magazine) yoghurts. Or Lynx hairdressing salons.

Another facet of brand extension is the 'sub-brand', which describes a kind of child of the original brand. Again, there are potentially real benefits in giving the new brand a kick-start in the marketplace, but there are also dangers. Walkers have had great success with their Sensations sub-brand, but have not done as well with other extensions. Cadbury's opened hot-chocolate shops and then closed them. PG opened tea-shops and then closed them.

Sometimes it's a matter of what marketing theorists call 'permission'. Cadbury's have our permission to make chocolate and drinking chocolate (and in fact to have a whole raft of sub-brands, from Dairy Milk to Crunchie). What they don't have our 'permission' to do is to run hot-chocolate shops. Possibly in part because we don't really understand what a 'hot-chocolate' shop is for.

Supermarkets have successfully sold insurance and finance products, of course. How? Because we associate supermarkets with convenience, speed and value. And because some of us don't want to think too much about our financial bits and pieces. So, although the leap from food to finance is big, we give them 'permission' to do it because we can see the benefit to us as consumers.

M&S food halls are much admired. Pretty classy food, sometimes with some real bargains. And we might occasionally have an 'out shopping' coffee-break in M&S. And they have done very well opening M&S food outlets in motorway service areas and railway stations. But it's hard to imagine going to M&S for an evening meal. It's just wrong emotionally.

Carluccios is both a restaurant, café and delicatessen: it succeeds because its whole purpose from the beginning has been to celebrate and serve Italian food with panache and style. Very single-minded; and that single-mindedness can be 'extended' into food products and even into kitchenware and cookery books.

Adnams (featured elsewhere in this book) has successfully stretched itself from being a brewer and pub owner to running cafés, wine stores and even kitchenware. All without damaging the brand: in fact, enhancing it at every careful but bold step because Adnams has stuck single-mindedly to its values and its brand story.

Brand extensions won't work if the link is tenuous, or seems contrived or desperate. Or if you simply don't have 'permission' to be in the new market. Levi's has permission to provide jeans, t-shirts, belts and related bits and pieces. It would never have permission to make suits (and, believe it or not, it tried and failed).

 One final thought. Who would have guessed that coffee shops inside bookshops would be a success? But they are. Not as brand extensions though, and that's the interesting bit. I wouldn't trust Waterstones to make me coffee. But I trust them to allow Costa and Starbucks to do so.

Brand Builder Workout

This workout will really only apply to you if you already have a cunning plan at the back of your mind to extend your brand or to create one or more sub-brands. Alternatively, if you're already in business, you might like to think about any existing brand extensions and sub-brands using the same questions.

So, before you do anything, think about the following.

- Why do you want to extend your brand? Is it because you see a real opportunity? Or is it because you are reacting to what someone else is doing? Or are you just getting bored and restless with your existing brand? Or are you panicking? (Trust me, brand extension is not a cure for panic.)

- Is there a natural (logical and emotional) link between your existing brand's product or service and the new project? In other words, will it make sense to customers?

- Even if the new project is potentially a great idea, does it really need to use the existing brand? Perhaps it would be better to start a completely new and fresh brand for this new project?

- Does your existing brand have customer 'permission' to operate in this new market place. Remember the examples above?

- Might a failure of the new extension actually damage the existing brand?

If the answers to all these questions are satisfactory and you still want to create a brand-extension... then please go back and ask them again because I'm still not convinced!

REAL BRAND STORY

What makes Pret special?

Jay Chapman, Head of Communications at Pret A Manger, explains why Pret doesn't do brand training with its staff, or even use the word 'brand'.

First, I'm not going to reveal a complicated, tailor-made formula for our success because there isn't one. To pretend that such a thing exists pays an enormous disservice to the efforts of everyone at Pret to keep things simple and non-formulaic.

I'm very aware that this is my contribution to a book all about branding, so admitting to a personal dislike of the word 'brand' might seem like an odd starting position. We don't have anyone at Pret with that word in their job title. I think as soon as you have official 'brand people' then it sends a message to the wider company that the brand is someone else's responsibility when in fact it's everyone's responsibility. Everything you do as a business affects the way your customers see you, and companies would do well to acknowledge this. We try to concentrate our efforts on making sure that the points at which our customers interact with us are as positive and engaging as they can be. At Pret, those key points are our *food* and our *people*.

We're a food company so the focus on *food* shouldn't be too much of a surprise to anyone. (Although the test kitchen in Hudson's Place – what we call our head office – does surprise lots of people when they visit us). Again, our approach to our food is pretty simple. We source the best ingredients we can find (we don't mind that our fresh, fragile ingredients go off quickly), we stay firmly committed to our mission statement (preservative free, all natural food), we build kitchens in the vast majority of our shops (so we can make our food fresh throughout the day) and what we don't sell, we give away to charity (because throwing good food away and wasting hard work make no sense). No rocket science here; in fact, our customers could easily make their own Pret food. If they had the time. If they had a full fridge. If they had the passion.

When it comes to our people, I often get asked about our brand training, i.e. how we get all of our team members to 'live the brand' so effectively. Once again, I feel slightly embarrassed that the answer is so simple. We don't do any brand training. I couldn't show you a single book or manual or training course or interactive module containing those words.

The truth is, we just recruit the right people and then look after them. We don't recruit experienced sandwich makers and then teach them to smile and be personable to our customers. We recruit smiley, personable people and teach them how to make sandwiches. Our recruitment process is rigorous and involves the candidate working a shift in one of our shop kitchens and the rest of the team voting on his or her suitability. This is a hugely powerful part of the process as it gives shared ownership of the decisions about who joins us.

Many of our team members are in their early 20s, lots are from overseas and are working with us whilst they improve their English. We know this. And we don't try and pretend that it's any different. We accept that (for example) Pret's 3-year strategic goals are going to be of limited use as a motivational tool. Instead, we incentivize them with things that resonate with them and their lives: cash and alcohol!

Cash? Well, every Pret shop is 'mystery shopped' each week and if they pass all of the criteria (immaculately clean shops, fantastic food selection, amazing, attentive service, etc., etc), each Team Member (TM) gets an additional £1 for every hour they've worked that week. The extra cash goes straight in their pockets.

And alcohol? Every month we host 'Friday Night Drinks' where we hire a central London venue (our regional shops do their own things locally) and invite all our TMs. We put some money behind the bar and all drinks are £1. The subsidized drinks are gratefully and very happily received.

These are just two of the ways that we motivate and keep our shop teams happy. There are lots more.

We serve delicious food using top quality ingredients served by people that care. It's as simple as that. We firmly believe that if we protect the integrity of our food and look after our people... then the brand will look after itself.

Day 30

NEXT STEPS

You're on a journey now. A brand journey. And short of discovering new territories on Earth or exploring space I can't think of many more stimulating journeys. People start businesses for a host of different reasons. The need to make a living might be paramount, but not necessarily so. There are many safer and less stressful ways to make a living than starting your own business. If starting a business is challenging, then creating a brand is more so. Where the disciplines of business are generally those of the head (rational, measurable, and to a certain extent predictable), those of creating a brand are fundamentally of the heart and soul (intuitive, not measurable by normal means, and always unpredictable).

Creating and building a brand will always be an endeavour of love, because brands are themselves about 'meaning', about wants rather than needs, about dreams and aspirations, and desires, and loyalty and ambition and hope and imagination.

So you've begun your brand journey and I hope this book has been useful and supportive to you along the way.

My best advice for the next steps is simply this: remember always that your brand doesn't really belong to you. It belongs to all those people for whom you have created meaning. It might be a meaning about something ever so humble. But it is meaning nevertheless, and it is that meaning which keeps them coming back to you rather than going somewhere else. It's not really a question of 'loyalty'. I don't believe in 'brand loyalty'. Labradors are loyal, but I'm not sure we are very Labrador-like. Blind loyalty is not what us brand-builders seek to engender. Instead we want people to 'love' our brand. Love is a big want, isn't it? But it's love that will set your business or organization apart from others.

Keep thinking about what your brand 'means' to the people who love it, and what it could mean to the people who haven't yet fallen in love with it, and you will never be far from the path. And before we finish there is one last exercise. Actually you've done this exercise already, but you've come a long way since then.

Good luck.

Brand Builder Workout

Put yourself in the shoes of your customers today, and try to write down your brand meaning as they would see it. And when you think you've captured this, go back and compare this list to the set of meanings you wrote down on day 1.

Meaning 1: _____

Meaning 2: _____

Meaning 3: _____

Meaning 4: _____

Meaning 5: _____

Meaning 6: _____

MY REAL BRAND STORY

Hemsby & Newport, Norfolk

A story from me this time, and one close to my heart: showing how a bit of imagination can make a brand come alive.

In March 2009 I got a phone call from James Gray, owner of Lost World Mini-Golf, a small attraction in the tiny seaside resort of Hemsby & Newport on the Norfolk coast, just 25 miles from my home in Norwich.

Hemsby is what most people would call a traditional or even an old-fashioned seaside resort. A magnificent long sandy beach faces the tumbling North Sea, and behind the dunes lies a little resort of cafés, various amusements and attractions and some beach-holiday oriented shops.

Hemsby & Newport (two settlements making in effect one resort) has been hosting holidaymakers for at least a century. But in recent years its fortunes have dwindled as the resort has been hit, like so many others, by the impact of cheap flights, the perception of unpredictable weather (although in actuality Norfolk is England's driest county), and changing holiday tastes.

The core of Hemsby's holiday accommodation is provided by low-cost chalets, many of them in holiday parks. Most of the chalets are owned by individuals or by small family firms who run several such parks at the resort. The only big player in Hemsby was Pontins, which closed their 1300 bed park in the resort at the end of the 2008 season. The loss of so many beds (translating directly into spending visitors to the resort) seemed like the final blow for several of the resort's traders, and spirits were low. But an informal group of the traders, among them James Gray, decided to fight back.

They made two important 'brand' decisions. One was to actively engage with the tourism agency of the much larger resort of Gt Yarmouth, seeking the GYTA's support in marketing the resort. The second was to realise that Hemsby actually had a 'brand' problem and not just a marketing one. Hence the phone call I received from James Gray.

I had holidayed in Hemsby a couple of times as a child, and taken my children there for days out when they were little. But I hadn't returned there for years and that, it turned out, was not unusual. Carrying out some very informal research about the place, I was frequently told, "Oh yes, Hemsby's a great little place, haven't been there for years."

The traders of Hemsby & Newport were straight with me from the start: there was no money to pay for my involvement. But it's hard to resist a challenge like the one they faced, so I agreed to propose a strategy on the proviso that they listened seriously to my suggestions.

I knew from the outset that the task wasn't about changing Hemsby (there's nothing wrong with a traditional, low-cost, English seaside holiday), but rather about raising its profile and enhancing its reputation. The challenge was to try to do this with virtually no budget.

As you know from the rest of this book, I am a passionate believer in the power of story to make an impact on brand reputation, and here was a perfect test of my theory. But what was the story? Well, it didn't take long to find it. A small amount of desk research revealed that the suffix 'by' at the end of Hemsby is a Viking word meaning farm or settlement. Local received wisdom is that the beaches of east Norfolk were landed by Norse invaders around 1200 years ago. Archaeologists say there's no evidence for this, but I maintain that absence of evidence is far from being evidence of absence, and I certainly wasn't going to let gaps in the archaeological record stand in the way of a good story.

So my core proposal to the traders of Hemsby was to celebrate and bring to life the idea that the first people to have fun on the beach at Hemsby were Vikings, which led in turn to a fantastic new logo for the resort featuring a cheery Viking waving a bucket and spade (instead of axe and shield), and a new positioning line: 1200 years of seaside fun.

The logo was designed (also *pro bono*) by Scott Poulson at Special Design Studio, another genuine fan of the resort. It has subsequently been used on the resort's cheery welcoming sign, on postcards, on the new website www.hemsbynorfolk.co.uk and has had widespread media coverage.

But it's one thing to develop a new narrative like this, and another to bring it to life. So I suggested that the Viking story be celebrated in real style with an annual Viking Festival. In fact I suggested a 'Scandinavian' festival, but it was quite rightly pointed out to me by the traders (rapidly becoming very brand savvy) that it was the word 'Viking' which had the real power to evoke drama, excitement and interest.

So the Hemsby & Newport Viking Festival (the first of its kind in Norfolk) will take place on the third weekend of June every year.

For a relatively modest idea this Viking story has had astonishing impact. Local BBC and ITV news have covered it. The regional daily paper and local weekly press have featured it extensively. London's free newspaper *Metro* has covered it in a double page feature. The Hemsby story has been featured in the marketing industry magazine *Marketing Week* as an example of destination branding in action. I have even been invited to speak about the project at a major international tourism conference in Stockholm.

The Viking theme and the festival have made a real impact on morale and determination amongst the traders of the resort, which proves that brand can play a role in changing the way people 'inside' a brand think and feel, as well as those outside. But I knew the Viking story wasn't enough to really get the brand perceptions of Hemsby moving from the off. Something extra was required. Something that gave a real sense of pride, optimism and new focus. This is where fabulous Norfolk-based travel photographer Ian Aitken stepped in, also (remarkably) agreeing to work on the Hemsby project free of charge.

Ian and I worked out a brief together, which led to him creating an extraordinary and unique collection of portraits of the resort, featuring photographs of local people and their businesses. The pictures captured many different moods, but all showed a fierce pride in the resort (which I like to think has echoes of a kind of Viking spirit). The portrait collection was exhibited in a Norwich art gallery and at the headquarters of Visit Britain in Regent Street, London, gaining yet more media coverage for the resort.

The arm-twisting of friends wasn't finished there, though. Martin Kentish of Free Range People also worked *pro bono*, creating an instant customer feedback mechanism for visitors. More than 20 traders are taking part in the programme, which invites customers to pick up a postcard in shop, café or attraction with a phone number to which they can text instant feedback (and a score out of 10) about the service received. Feedback is sent instantly to the proprietor who can thank the customer by return. This scheme won still further media coverage, and demonstrated that Hemsby was committed to providing a great customer experience.

Finally, I managed to persuade Nik Coleman at Treefrog Television, my co-producer on the TV series 'The Brand Effect' to feature the resort in its own special episode. Currently in production, that programme provides further news interest and keeps the Hemsby & Newport profile high.

The marketing literature produced in cooperation with the Gt Yarmouth Tourism Authority and the independently created website completes the jigsaw of brand efforts for Hemsby & Newport. Energy levels, optimism and determination to succeed are now high amongst the traders of the resort: and they will succeed because, fundamentally, they realized that the challenge they faced was indeed a 'brand' challenge.

REFERENCES AND RECOMMENDED READING

If this book has inspired you to explore the power of branding a little deeper, you might like to dip into some of these books. None of them is academic (though there are plenty of those and some of them are excellent, of course). Everything here is accessible and stimulating for anyone who takes the brand of their business or organization seriously. You don't need any marketing education or training: just an open mind.

And if you had to pick just two out of the whole list... I'd go with Kevin Roberts on *Lovemarks* and Seth Godin's classic *Purple Cow*.

A reading list is pretty much doomed to be out of date before it's even published, but this is a pretty good starting point for anyone who wants brand insight without too much academic research or theory. Apart from their other merits all of these books are, in their own way, fun. Honest.

It's Not How Good You Are, It's How Good You Want To Be, Paul Arden, Phaidon, 2003. Not about branding at all, but a punchy and thought-provoking little read all the same. A great little inspiration for brand owners, entrepreneurs and self-starters of all kinds. And nicely presented (it's actually something of a brand in its own right, in fact).

Web Marketing for Small Businesses, Stephanie Diamond, Source-books, 2008. A step-by-step 'how to' on web marketing by one of the contributors to this book. Not to be read in isolation, because the web changes all the time, so this kind of book is always going to be very time sensitive. Nevertheless, if you like the style, very useful in helping you to express your brand online.

The Tipping Point, Malcolm Gladwell, Little, Brown, 2000. Gladwell is controversial and so are his ideas, but this, his breakthrough book, is a compelling read and delivers a very exciting thought to brand owners no matter how small: that from even the humblest of beginnings things (given the right set of circumstances) can reach a 'tipping point' and get very big indeed.

All Marketers Are Liars: the power of telling authentic stories in a low-trust world, Seth Godin, Penguin, 2006. It's all in the sub-title: a book about telling authentic stories for brand success, and about the immense difficulty (not to say futility) of trying to get people to 'change' their mindsets. Don't even try, says Godin: there are better ways to market your brand.

Purple Cow, Seth Godin, Penguin, 2005. A classic. Easy to read, engaging, inspiring and invaluable. Packed with great stories about truly distinctive brand behaviour. A must-read of branding for entrepreneurs if ever there was one.

Small is the New Big, Seth Godin, Penguin, 2006. Seth's third entry in my recommended reading list (you can tell I'm a fan) is not a brand book *per se*: but it's a heck of an exhilarating ride for any brand owner who wants to have their own comfort-zone constantly challenged. Just dip in anywhere in this collection of 184 short essays and I defy you not to want to improve something about your business!

The Brand Innovation Manifesto, John Grant, John Wiley & Sons Ltd,, 2006. A book really aimed at the corporate brand manager rather than the entrepreneur, but a fascinating and useful book neverthe-less, most notable for Grant's brilliant 'periodic table of brand ideas' which I have used to help numerous clients understand and identify their most powerful brand stories.

Made to Stick: why some ideas take hold and others come unstuck, Dan Heath and Chip Heath, Arrow, 2008. A brilliant analysis of the es-sentials of a great brand story and how to craft yours so that it really 'sticks'. Starting with a terrifying urban legend, this is a book that really sticks.

ZAG: the no. 1 strategy of high-performance brands, Marty Neumeier, New Riders, 2007/ A one-idea look at brands, but it's a big and im-portant idea: that the most important thing you have to achieve is being different. Really different. Easy to read and instantly inspiring, though I think only part of the story.

The 22 Immutable Laws of Branding, Al Ries and Laura Ries, Harper Collins, 1999. Well, I'm not sure anything is immutable: but this is nevertheless an important and enormously helpful touchstone of a book. Short and easy to read and always rewarding to revisit when you're reviewing how your brand is progressing. Always refer to this book when you're considering brand changes, extensions, etc.!

Positioning: the battle for your mind, Al Ries and Jack Trout, McGraw-Hill, 2001. Rightly called a marketing classic, this is a brilliant captur-ing and explanation of the big subject of 'brand positioning' which Ries and Trout 'invented' through legendary magazine articles in 1972. The positioning concept has acquired a mystical aura in the subsequent decades.

Lovemarks: the future beyond brands, Kevin Roberts, Powerhouse Cultural Entertainment Books, revised edition 2006. A brilliant model by the global head of Saatchi & Saatchi, which anyone can, and probably everyone should, apply to their brand at least once. Are you a Lovemark? Find out out here.

The Lovemarks Effect: winning in the consumer revolution, Kevin Roberts, Powerhouse Cultural Entertainment Books, 2006. The sequel to the brilliant original *Lovemarks* book, this one features a host of case studies and contributions from brand owners, fans and commentators including Tom Peters. Hugely inspiring for all brand owners everywhere.

The Viking Manifesto: the Scandinavian approach to business and blasphemy, Steve Srid and Claes Andreasson, Cyan, 2007. A book about business 'behaviour' rather than specifically about branding: but as you know I believe brands are fundamentally about behaviour and the meanings it creates. Light and easy to read, but with a healthy dose of inspiringly subversive brand ideas. Brand like a Viking!

I'm With the Brand, Rob Walker, Constable, 2008. In which we discover that not only do we use brands to make sense of our world, but if brands didn't exist we'd invent them all over again because they give us something that we need as humans. A great analysis of how some brands achieve the status of people wanting to 'embrace' them and become active advocates for them.

Brand Hijack: marketing without marketing, Alex Wipperfürth, Portfolio, 2005. A dense and challenging read, but potentially very powerful, this book proposes letting your 'customers' take over your marketing for you,based on the core philosophy that you don't really own your brand at all, the 'people' do.

REAL BRAND STORY AND EXPERT VIEW CONTRIBUTORS

Andy Wood, Adnams plc, *www.adnams.co.uk*

Bea Hatherley, Mr. Site, *www.mrsite.co.uk*

Brian Horner, Voluntary Norfolk, *www.voluntarynorfolk.org.uk*

Caroline Rust, WorkShopsWork, *www.workshopswork.co.uk*

Chris Murphy, Balloon Dog, *www.balloondog.co.uk*

David Keeling, bpha, *www.bpha.org.uk*

David Knights and Robert Spigel, Anthony Nolan, *www.anthonynolan.org.uk*

Fiona Ryder, StreamExchange, *www.streamexchange.co.uk*

Gordon Maw, MAW Communications, *www.mawcomms.co.uk*

Jay Chapman, Pret A Manger, *www.pret.com*

Jess Morgan, *www.jessmorgan.co.uk*

Mark Cook, Further Search Marketing, *www.further.co.uk*

Sarah Pettegree, Bray's Cottage Farm, *www.perfectpie.co.uk*

Scott Poulson, Special Design Studio, *www.specialdesignstudio.com*

Simon Egan and Tom Blofeld and John Lyle, BeWILDerwood, *www. bewilderwood.com*

Stephanie Diamond, Digital Media Works, *www.digmediaworks.com*

Tracy Kenny, *www.tracykenny.co.uk*

BRAND STRATEGY GURU SPEAKING AND CONSULTANCY

Simon Middleton personally presents master classes, seminars, keynotes and bespoke workshops on the topics covered in this book. For more information visit www.brandstrategyguru.com.

He also fronts a kick-ass acoustic-roots Americana band and you can see his other side at www.thepropositionband.com!

Thanks for reading.

INDEX